The Texas Secession. The Mexican War. The Gadsden Purchase. By the time the dust had settled, one-half of what used to be Mexico had become one-third of what is now the United States, and a full century of bad feelings was inevitable.

But the lopsided algebra of Mexico-U.S. relations has been transformed. Our complex world no longer respects national boundaries, and the destinies of the United States and Mexico are merging. Indeed, the border that really separates North America's two most populous countries today is not physical, but cultural. *The Disappearing Border: Mexico–United States Relations to the 1990s*—replete with maps, tables, historical photographs, and reproductions of Mexican art—tells you what you need to know to bridge that gap.

Clint E. Smith, career diplomat and consulting professor of Latin American studies at Stanford University, has been focusing on Latin American affairs for the better part of the past three decades.

THE DISAPPEARING
BORDER

Mexico–United States Relations to the 1990s

by

Clint E. Smith

THE PORTABLE STANFORD is a book series
sponsored by the Stanford Alumni Association.
The series is designed to bring the widest possible
sampling of Stanford's intellectual resources into the
homes of alumni. It includes books based on current
research as well as books that deal with philosophical
issues, which by their nature reflect to a greater degree
the personal views of their authors.

THE PORTABLE STANFORD BOOK SERIES
Stanford Alumni Association
Bowman Alumni House
Stanford, California 94305-4005

Library of Congress Catalog Card
Number: 92-060483
ISBN: 0-916318-50-8

10 9 8 7 6 5 4 3 2 1

The
Portable Stanford
Book Series

Published by the
Stanford Alumni Association

Editor-in-chief: Della van Heyst
Series Editor and Manager: Bruce Goldman
Book Design/Production Manager: Amy Pilkington
Cover Design: David Rose
Cover Art: Jeffrey Adams

DEDICATION

To Marilyn Sode Smith.
With Love and Appreciation.

ACKNOWLEDGMENTS

A great many scholars, government officials, businessmen, bankers, artists, writers, students, and others on both sides of the "disappearing border" have helped me over the last few decades to learn something about the fascinating and complex nature of the relationship between Mexico and the United States. Several of these friends and colleagues have already written about Mexico and the United States, and their works are to be found in the Reader's Guide at the end of this volume. These works are rich in insight and represent a very broad range of views and approaches to the U.S.-Mexico relationship, and I consulted them frequently in the preparation of this book. They are generally fuller in scope or deeper in focus than my brief volume; perhaps a principal accomplishment of this study is to invite these works to your attention. I commend them to you, and hope that the authors will understand the impossibility of singling them out individually on this page.

I also want to thank those former students who have contributed to my understanding of the relationship, and especially those who, thanks to support by the Center for Latin American Studies, have assisted me in researching this book. These include Guadalupe Paz, Curtis Vredenburg, and Robin Linsenmayer. I am particularly appreciative of the kindness of Robert Ryal Miller, professor emeritus of history and an eminent historian of Mexico, who offered useful suggestions after reading the first draft of the early chapters of this volume. I also thank my editor at the Portable Stanford, Bruce Goldman, and production manager and book designer Amy Pilkington, for their skilled assistance. I take full responsibility for any errors that have crept in despite everyone's best efforts.

I also want to thank William R. Hewlett, chairman of the board, and Roger W. Heyns, president, of The William and Flora Hewlett Foundation, for their early recognition of the importance of United States–Mexico policy studies and for their support of this work at a number of leading institutions in both countries over the past decade. It is a pleasure for me to be associated with them in these efforts.

Finally, I want everyone to know that without the initial encouragement and steadfast support of my wife, Marilyn Sode Smith, it would have been impossible for me to write this book.

TABLE OF
CONTENTS

CHRONOLOGY xv
INTRODUCTION xxiii

PART I
1. TWO YOUNG COUNTRIES (1800–1910) 1

The Colonial Period 1
The Mexican Struggle for Independence 6
Independence: The Early Years 7
The Fight for Texas 9
The War of the North American Invasion 14
The Presidency of Benito Juárez: A New Era Begins 18
Early Mexican Victory at Puebla: The "Cinco de Mayo" ... 19
The Unhappy Reign of Emperor Maximilian 20
Mexico Enters the Modern Age 24
The Porfiriato: 1876–1910 25

2. THE COSMIC RACE (1910–24) 31

The Short, Sad Term of Francisco I. Madero 37
The Huerta Regime and Woodrow Wilson 39
The *Dolphin* Incident 40
Carranza and the Constitution of 1917 42
Alvaro Obregón and the Beginnings of Peace 46
Relations with the U.S. Under Obregón 48

3. Mexico Grows and Develops (1924–Present) 51
    Calles Creates a Structure for Governance........................... 51
    Cárdenas, Roosevelt, and the Oil Crisis 55
    The U.S. and Mexico in World War II 57
    The Postwar Years 60
    López Mateos, Cuba, and Chamizal.................................. 63
    President Díaz Ordaz and the Tlatelolco Massacre............. 65
    The Echeverría Years.. 66
    José López Portillo: Oil, Debt, and Corruption 69
    De la Madrid: A Period of Patient Rebuilding 72
    Salinas de Gortari: Mexico Prepares for the 21st Century . 75
    A Giant Step Forward in Social Reform............................. 79
    The August 1991 Elections and Beyond 81

PART II

4. United States-Mexico Foreign Relations 85
    A Matter of Perspective 86
    Mexico and the World 89
    The Oil Binge 92
    The Hazing of Jimmy Carter 95
    Sobering Up 97

5. Drugs, Rivers, and Dolphins: Striking a Balance 101
    Drug Trafficking.. 101
    The International Boundary and Water Commission 108
    Trade, Ecology, and Dolphins 110
    Three Concrete Recommendations 112

6. "Controlling" Migration 115
    The U.S.-Mexico Dimension 116
    The Numbers Game... 122
    U.S. Debate on Immigration Reform: 1970–86.................. 122
    The Immigration Reform and Control Act of 1986 123
    Current Migration Flows 126
    Three Red Herrings: Worker Displacement,
        Welfare Abuse, and Cultural Separatism........................ 128

7. Toward an Economic Partnership 131
A Twelve-Year Decline in Relations Begins 133
De la Madrid and Salinas Embark on Economic and
    Political Reform 133
Salinas Expands Internal Reform, U.S. Trade Relations ... 134
The Mexican Foreign Investment Boom 136
Oil Remains a Sensitive Issue 140
A Parallel Process of Political Reform 141
The Mexican Debt: From Crisis to Resolution 141
Agrarian Reform in 1992 144
Economic Partnership 146

PART III

8. The North American Free Trade Agreement 151
Background and History 151
The North American Market Economy 154
NAFTA: The Basic Issues 158
Canada and the NAFTA Debate 162
NAFTA and the Environment 162
Confusing International Negotiations with Intervention . 164
The Roots of Opposition to NAFTA: An Assessment 164
NAFTA's Global Implications 166
Preparing for the 21st Century 168

Reader's Guide 171
About the Author 175
Backlist 177

Chronology of Events

1810	Mexican war of independence begins.
	Father Miguel Hidalgo y Costilla proclaims Mexican independence from Spain on September 16.
1811	Hidalgo captured and executed by Spanish.
1821	Conservative forces led by former Spanish officer Agustín de Iturbide secure Mexican independence from Spain.
1822	Iturbide crowned Emperor Agustín I.
	Mexico annexes Central America.
	Texan politician Stephen Austin granted permission to settle U.S. colonists in Texas.
1823	Iturbide forced to abdicate. Central America secedes from Mexico.
1824	First constitution drafted. Guadalupe Victoria elected first president of Mexico.
1828	Mexico abolishes slavery in attempt to discourage Anglo settlement of Texas.
1830	Mexican government bans further American settlement of Texas.
1834	Texas secedes from Mexico.
1836	Mexican general Antonio López de Santa Anna arrives in Texas with an army. He storms the Alamo but is defeated and captured at San Jacinto by rebellious Texans and forced to grant Texas independence.
1845	United States annexes Texas.
1846	Border skirmishes lead to United States declaration of war on Mexico.

1847   Gen. Zachary Taylor decisively defeats Mexican forces at Angostura.

U.S. Army expeditionary force under General Winfield Scott lands at Veracruz and then takes Mexico City.

1848   Mexico signs Treaty of Guadalupe Hidalgo. In exchange for $15 million, Mexico cedes California, Nevada, Arizona, New Mexico, Utah, and part of Colorado to the United States.

1853   United States purchases large tract of southern New Mexico and Arizona from Mexico for railroad expansion. Known as the Gadsden Purchase.

1857   Mexico's Liberal government adopts a new constitution, limiting church power and broadening individual freedoms.

Conservatives stage a revolt and take Mexico City.

Benito Juárez leads Liberal forces.

1860   Liberal victory: Juárez recaptures Mexico City and becomes first full-blooded Indian president of Mexico.

1861   Spanish, British, and French forces occupy Veracruz demanding repayment of debts.

1862   Britain and Spain withdraw troops, but French drive inland and are defeated on May 5 (cinco de mayo) at Puebla.

1863   French troops drive Juárez from the Mexican capital.

1864   France installs Maximilian as emperor of Mexico.

1867   Maximilian executed; Juárez reelected president.

1876   Juárez's successor, Sebastian Lerdo de Tejada, overthrown by Gen. Porfirio Díaz.

Díaz begins 34-year rule (except for 1880–4). Extensive U.S. investment in Mexico, especially in railroads and mining.

1910   Moderate Francisco Madero proclaims Plan of San Luis Potosí, calling for revolt against Díaz and free elections. Beginning of

Mexican Revolution as rebellions break out in the north and in Puebla.

1911 After 34 years of rule, Díaz resigns in the face of expanding rebellions and sails to France.

Madero returns from exile in the United States and is elected president.

Emiliano Zapata, in south, declares Madero a traitor and drafts Plan of Ayala, calling for land redistribution.

1913 Ten Tragic Days, February 8–18. Madero and Vice President Jesús María Pino Suárez arrested and killed on orders of Gen. Victoriano Huerta. U.S. ambassador Henry Lane Wilson, a critic of Madero, is indirectly implicated. President Woodrow Wilson refuses to recognize Huerta's government and brings economic and diplomatic pressure on Huerta.

Pancho Villa and Venustiano Carranza, in north, and Emiliano Zapata, in south, all take up arms against Huerta.

1914 U.S. Naval forces seize Veracruz to deprive Huerta of arms shipments and stay for seven months.

Huerta flees Mexico, and Carranza's forces under Gen. Alvaro Obregón take Mexico City. (Huerta dies two years later in an El Paso jail).

Revolutionary convention at Aguascalientes adopts Plan of Ayala.

World War I begins in Europe in August.

U.S. soldiers withdraw from Veracruz.

1915 Villa defeated at Celaya, but continues to fight.

Carranza recognized by the United States as chief of government forces.

1916 Villa raids town of Columbus, New Mexico. U.S. army sends punitive force under Gen. John Pershing into Mexico in search of Villa.

Carranza's forces invade Morelos, center of Zapata's support.

1917 Pershing withdraws from Mexico, having failed to find Villa.

Carranza's government adopts the Constitution of 1917, providing for labor and land reform.

Carranza elected constitutional president.

United States enters World War I in April.

German foreign minister, Arthur Zimmerman, sends telegram to Carranza offering to restore all territories lost to U.S. in Mexican War in exchange for Mexico's support. Carranza rejects offer.

1919 Last U.S. incursion into Mexico, after Villa attacks Ciudad Juárez.

1920 Carranza's regime toppled; he flees Mexico City and is killed.

Obregón becomes president.

Villa ends his rebellion.

1921 José Vasconcelos becomes minister of education and starts cultural and literacy campaigns.

1923 United States and Mexico sign Bucareli Agreements, guaranteeing sanctity of U.S. property in Mexico in exchange for United States recognition of Obregón's government.

Villa assassinated.

1924 United States gives Obregón arms to suppress a coup.

Mexico recognizes the Soviet Union.

Plutarco Elías Calles elected president.

1926 Calles's anticlerical policies lead to the Cristero Rebellion, an uprising of priests and peasants.

1927 Ambassador Dwight Morrow is sent to Mexico to negotiate petroleum disputes; he also helps in mediation of church-state conflicts.

1928   Calles succeeded by Obregón; Obregón is assassinated in July.

Calles begins six-year reign as *jefe político*, selecting functionary presidents, the first of whom is Emilio Portes Gil.

1929   Founding of *Partido Nacional Revolucionario* (PNR).

Cristero Rebellion suppressed.

Calles, who remains political strongman through 1935, chooses Portes Gil as president.

1930   United States begins to deport Mexican workers.

1934   Lázaro Cárdenas becomes president, with support of workers, peasants, and leading elements of military.

1936   Cárdenas sends Calles into exile. The president arms 60,000 peasants to support his sweeping land reforms.

1938   Cárdenas nationalizes oil industry. United States responds with economic sanctions.

1939–42   *Partido Acción Nacional* (PAN) founded.

1940   Manuel Avila Camacho becomes president, promotes closer ties with U.S.

1941   United States enters World War II in December.

1942   Mexico enters World War II on Allied side in May.

United States and Mexico initiate *bracero* program, allowing Americans to contract Mexican agricultural labor.

1945   Inter-American Conference on Problems of War and Peace at Chapultepec.

1946   Miguel Alemán elected president.

Mexican industrialization intensifies.

Ruling party renamed *Partido Revolucionario Institucional*, or PRI.

1947   Harry Truman visits Mexico; Alemán tours Washington, D.C., New York, and Kansas City.

1952   Adolfo Ruiz Cortines succeeds Alemán.

United States deports illegal Mexican workers, so-called "Operation Wetback."

1958   Adolfo López Mateos elected president.

U.S.-Mexico trade and investment grow.

1964   Mexico and United States settle Chamizal boundary dispute, which arose in 1864 when the Rio Grande changed its course and passed 440 acres of Mexican territory to the U.S. side of the river.

1965   Border Industrialization Program created by Mexican government.

1968   Prior to Mexico City's hosting of Olympics, government brutally cracks down on leftist student demonstrations; hundreds of demonstrators massacred at Tlatelolco.

1970   Luis Echeverría elected president. The foreign policy activism and "Mexicanization" investment policies of the Echeverría government stimulate a significant downturn in U.S. relations with Mexico.

1974   Mexico joins Venezuela in creating a Latin American economic system.

1976   José López Portillo assumes presidency. During the early years of his term, high oil revenues bring record growth to Mexican economy and stimulate massive borrowing by government.

1977   The government launches electoral reform in face of growing voter apathy and criticism about the country's "one-party democracy." Chamber of Deputies increased to 400 seats to make room for opposition parties.

1979   Mexico breaks off relations with Nicaraguan dictator Anastasio Somoza and sides with Cuban-supported Sandinistas; also breaks previous promises and refuses to admit the terminally ill Shah of Iran following his ouster by fundamental Islamic forces. The two actions rankle the administration of U.S. president Jimmy Carter.

1980   After long negotiations, President López Portillo suddenly decides that Mexico will not join the General Agreement on Tariffs and Trade (GATT).

1981   Oil prices plummet late in year.

1982   Mexico forced to suspend payments on principal of foreign debt in August. Mexico's economic crises weaken Mexico's freedom to differ with Washington over economic and international issues.

López Portillo nationalizes banking system.

Miguel de la Madrid elected president. Mexico's massive foreign debt forces him to implement an economic stabilization program with austerity measures and to begin an extensive restructuring program.

1983   A wave of local victories by the center-right PAN raises new questions about the invincibility of the PRI government.

1985   Mexico City hit by devastating earthquake.

Slaying of DEA agent Enrique Camarena in Mexico strains U.S.-Mexican relations.

1986   Another electoral reform, designed in part to increase the government's credibility, increases the number of Chamber seats to 500, but conditions for effective multiparty democracy still not met.

Mexico joins the GATT, ushering in a new period of trade liberalization.

1987   Mexico and United States sign bilateral framework agreement for trade and investment.

A PRI faction called the Democratic Current leaves the party after the selection of technocrat Carlos Salinas de Gortari as presidential candidate. The Democratic Current, led by

Cuauhtémoc Cárdenas, goes on to form *Fronte Democrático Nacional* (FDN) to contest the 1988 presidential elections.

1988 Salinas defeats opposition candidate Cárdenas in presidential elections. Accusations of fraud lead to massive protests.

1989 *Partido Revolucionario Democrático* (PRD) formally founded, succeeding the FDN electoral coalition led by Cárdenas.

Mexico and the United States undertake bilateral Trade and Investment Facilitation Talks.

PAN wins first governorship in Baja California (Norte).

Constitutional amendment paves the way for electoral reforms.

Year-end agreements with multilateral lenders and commercial banks reduce Mexico's commercial debt and ease debt-service schedule.

1990 Presidents Bush and Salinas issue joint statement in June in support of negotiations for free-trade agreement.

1991 Canada joins negotiations for the establishment of a North American Free Trade Agreement (NAFTA) in February.

Congress allows fast-track NAFTA negotiations to proceed in June.

Large PRI plurality in 1991 midterm elections restores official party's stronghold in Congress. Next presidential election scheduled for 1994.

INTRODUCTION

"I, as a Mexican, am part of a singular paradox—that of Mexico and the United States. Our countries are neighbors, condemned to live alongside each other; they are separated, however, more by profound social, economic, and psychic differences than by physical and political frontiers."

❧ Octavio Paz

The 2,000-mile-long border shared by Mexico and the United States is practically unique in its separation of the First World from the Third. But that border is disappearing before our eyes: The "frontier" described by the great poet, philosopher, and Nobel laureate Octavio Paz has been rendered evanescent by a growing economic, political, social, and cultural interdependence.

In this book we explore the asymmetrical nature of that interdependent relationship and the sharp cultural and historical differences between the U.S. and Mexico: Paz's "singular paradox." During the earlier years of the relationship, this asymmetry—in industrial and technological capacity, in economic and military power—created an image of a weak Mexico dependent on the "Colossus of the North." Until the discovery of massive oil reserves in Mexico in the 1970s, a conventional description of the binational relationship would have stressed that country's alleged dependence on the United States and the "exploitative" role of U.S. and other transnational corporations; but no longer.

Moreover, the past decade has been marked by fundamental reforms in Mexico's economic and social structures; the rest of the world has changed, too. Importantly, several new or changing aspects of U.S.-Mexico relations—the debt crisis, narcotics trafficking, trade, and migration, just to name a few—have steered the U.S. in the direction of growing dependence on a stable and prosperous Mexico. This new era needs to be described, and a fresh look taken at the nature of the U.S.-Mexico relationship in the 1990s and beyond.

The U.S. and Mexico have arrived at their present circumstances by very different paths. Mexico's twin roots are embedded in a great Mesoamerican civilization—Mayan, Aztec, Zapotec—and in *la Madre Patria*—the mother country, Spain. The conflict between the two cultures resulted in a generally unhappy colonial experience and led to a 19th-century revolt against Spain—a rebellion catalyzed, ironically, by the growing strength of the *mestizo*, the very product of the two civilizations' intersection. The Mexican Revolution produced a system of one-party rule that has governed Mexico for more than sixty years, and, despite the electoral crisis of 1988, now seems poised to win the presidential elections in 1994.

The historical memories of the United States, which broke away from the Old World earlier and developed a democratic political system now two centuries old, are quite different. The result is two profoundly distinct perceptions, from the two sides of a disappearing border, of the major problems in the relationship.

Chapter 1 reviews several important early events: Anglo-American settlers' move to Texas (then a Mexican state); the Mexican War (or, to Mexicans, "The War of the North American Invasion"), which ended in Mexico's humiliation and loss of half its territory; the period of liberalization and reform as Mexico rebuilt afterward; and, finally, Mexico's emergence as an industrializing society.

Chapter 2 describes the onset of the Mexican Revolution and the long decade of violence and terror as opposing forces struggled for national power. Names almost magical in Mexican history books—Zapata, Pancho Villa, Carranza, Obregón—fill the pages of the story of this tragic decade (1910–20).

Chapter 3 catalogues the leading events in U.S.-Mexico relations from 1924 to the present. There is a focus on the controversial but still much-admired President Lázaro Cárdenas (1934–40), who is remembered for his efforts at land reform in Mexico's rural areas and for the expropriation of foreign oil companies. Special attention is paid to the administrations of the four most recent Mexican presidents—and particularly that of the current incumbent. President Carlos Salinas de Gortari's opening of the Mexican economy and liberal social programs have radically altered Mexico's domestic scene, improved relations with the U.S. and the world, and set the stage for the negotiation of a North American Free Trade Agreement and the creation of a North American community.

In Chapter 4 we identify and analyze the two countries' differing perspectives on foreign-policy issues. Chapter 5 looks at drug trafficking in the context of U.S.-Mexico relations; the International Boundary and Water Commission, a successful institution developed to deal with an important aspect of the bilateral relationship; and a typical, and current, bilateral dispute—the so-called "dolphin case." Because of the crime, violence, corruption, social disorder, individual destruction, and international tension it engenders, illicit drug trafficking constitutes a source of great tension between Mexico and the United States and is likely to remain so for at least the next decade. Perhaps in no other area has the intergovernmental relationship been more complex. The U.S. leadership has failed to attack the problem domestically on the demand side, while on its side of the border Mexico has been unable fully to curb illegal activities, sometimes involving civilian, police, and military officials.

Another matter of mutual concern—immigration—is not primarily a law enforcement issue. Mexican immigrants to the United States have by turns been welcomed with open arms and brusquely discouraged. Their growing numbers make Mexican-Americans a dynamic and positive presence in American society—particularly in the key states of California and Texas. Chapter 6 reviews patterns of migration throughout the entire history of the U.S.-Mexico relationship, but focuses on the period since the enactment of the Immigration Reform and Control Act of 1986. Given the U.S. and Mexico's rapidly growing economic and social interdependence, discussions parallel to the ongoing free-trade talks might be an ideal place to decriminalize migration and consider more seriously the underlying economic and social forces that affect North American labor flows.

In 1982 a new era of economic relations between the United States and Mexico began when Mexico's central bank ran out of foreign exchange, the foreign debt reached $100 billion, and a discredited outgoing president's nationalization of private banks and massive devaluations of the peso created a financial crisis that reverberated throughout Mexico and the world. Since then, the story has been one of rebuilding. Chapter 7 focuses on the 1980s and early 1990s, culminating in the dramatic economic strides of the Salinas administration. The chapter also highlights the recent growth of foreign investment in Mexico, President Salinas's reforms in agriculture and rural development, the current state of the binational relationship, and prospects for the 1990s and the 21st century.

Discussions of economic and social relations between the United States and Mexico are increasingly taking on a "North American" flavor, that of the inclusion of Canada in a vision of a united North American community. Chapter 8 explores the origins of the North American Free Trade Agreement now under negotiation, reviews the prospects for the continental community that may emerge over the coming decade or so, and looks ahead to the question of how best to manage the growing complexity of relations among the three major North American countries.

I have written this book as an introduction for the general reader, organized along the lines of the syllabus I use for my seminar on U.S.-Mexico relations at the Center for Latin American Studies at Stanford University. That syllabus, altered frequently over the years with the evolution of the relationship, has proven to be effective. But no short work such as this one can possibly encompass the full richness of the subject. That is why I urge you to refer often to the Reader's Guide, and to treat yourself to an in-depth look at subjects that particularly interest you.

PART I

HISTORY

1 Two Young Countries (1800–1910)

During the long period when the inhabitants of the thirteen English colonies and those of New Spain were engaged in their own struggles for independence (1775–83 for the United States, 1810–21 for Mexico), the two societies were small, and were separated from each other by a wide expanse of sparsely populated land.

One might be forgiven for thinking that relations between the two gestating nations would have been significant, as military confrontations between England and Spain had occurred sporadically since the 16th century. Colonists both in English America and New Spain looked on with concern as the major European powers fought, won, and lost wars and traded parts of the New World with each other. Cuba,

Florida, and Louisiana, pawns in this great game, were traded back and forth over the decades.

In fact, however, bilateral relations in the colonial period were marked by a mutual lack of interest and pervasive prejudice. While the colonists of New Spain looked askance at the religious reformers and heretics of the English colonies to the north, Cotton Mather prayed for (and even, in 1699, wrote a treatise on the need for) the spiritual regeneration of the benighted inhabitants of New Spain.

Not surprisingly, then, the two new North American nations took very different paths in their economic, social, and political development. They were guided largely by two quite distinct beginnings: The American colonies were settled in significant part by Puritans, Quakers, Catholics, and many others seeking religious freedom, who carried with them the seeds of political and economic liberalism that were to explode in the last quarter of the 18th century with the Declaration of Independence and the Constitution and its Bill of Rights. New Spain, on the other hand, was created by a process of armed exploration and political, economic, and religious conquest, which the Spanish *conquistadores* extended throughout the 16th century to Santa Fe and San Antonio and over the 17th and 18th centuries to Los Angeles, San Francisco, and beyond.

There was another important factor in the two countries' diverging paths toward development. In the American colonies, most of the indigenous peoples were typically driven away, and the villages and towns of the new colonists were largely populated by Europeans. The system of governance established in these towns, an outgrowth of Reformation England and the Continent, spread throughout the Colonies and grew more liberal and democratic in nature. The American economy became a free-enterprise system based on private initiative and ownership, in which the state, and certainly the church, played small roles. This combination of liberal political and economic systems

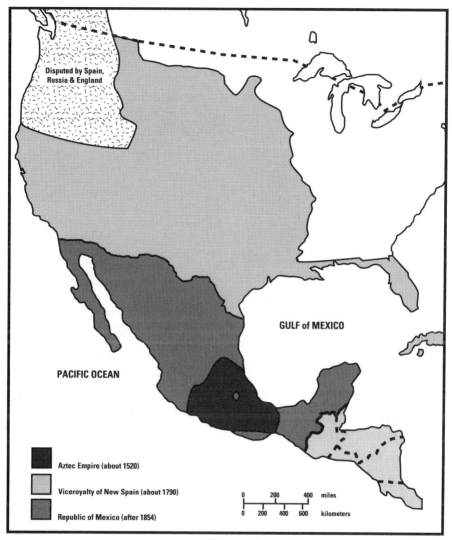

Figure 1.1
Extent of Aztec Empire, Viceroyalty, and Republic.

proved to be a powerful engine of growth for the new United States of America when it emerged late in the 18th century.

In contrast, the missionary priests who arrived in New Spain with the *conquistadores* labored to convert and co-opt the subjugated Aztecs, Mayans, Zapotecs, and other native peoples.

3

Indigenous labor soon became the vital support of the Viceregal economy in its sugar and wheat plantations, cattle ranches, gold and silver mines, and workshops. But although the social process in New Spain was inclusive in its co-optation of the indigenous peoples, it was also strictly hierarchical. Social privilege and political power were carefully measured by such criteria as one's rank in the Spanish nobility, the Church, the military, or the royal system of *encomiendas,* under which privileged *peninsulares* (Spaniards actually born in Spain) or *criollos* (Spaniards of "pure blood" born in New Spain) were given by the King's order a group of Indians "to care for"—which all too often meant "to exploit unmercifully."

Much lower in the hierarchy of New Spain was the rapidly growing population of *mestizos,* those born of mixed Spanish and Indian heritage. While accepted as foremen in the mines, plantations, ranches, and small factories or as skilled artisans and modest merchants, they did not enjoy the social status or power of the *criollos* or *peninsulares.* In 1800, the Mexican population of about 5 million was composed of some 2.5 million *indios,* 1 million *criollos* and *peninsulares,* and some 1.5 million *mestizos.* Although they accounted for only about 30 percent of the total in 1800, *mestizos* became the predominant element in Mexican society over the next century, emerging from the Mexican Revolution of 1910 as the central feature of modern Mexico's self-identity. It was this group that the Mexican philosopher and educator José Vasconcelos was later, in the aftermath of the revolution, to call *la raza cósmica* (the cosmic race, in recognition of the fact that the *mestizos* represented all the major "human races"—Caucasian, African, and Oriental—as perceived at that time).

This later view of the *mestizo* as the hallmark of Mexican self-perception was foreshadowed by the role *mestizos* played in the short, unhappy, but vitally important uprising in September 1810 by the *criollo* soldier-priest Father Hidalgo, one of the most

Figure 1.2
Hidalgo Initiates the War for Independence.
Mural by Juan O'Gorman.

revered figures in Mexican history.

While Father Hidalgo's rebellion was short-lived, his heroism and vision were vital precursors to the subsequent successful battles by another soldier-priest, Father José María Morelos, and many other heroes of the struggle for independence. This struggle came to a successful conclusion on September 28, 1821, with the ringing of church bells throughout Mexico City and the countryside to celebrate a peace treaty signed by the warring factions, and the installation of General Agustín Iturbide as the leader of the ruling military *junta*.

THE MEXICAN STRUGGLE FOR INDEPENDENCE

Miguel Hidalgo y Costilla was born of *criollo* parents who managed an *hacienda* near the village of Dolores in the province of Guanajuato. A champion of the *mestizo* and the *indio*, he was a popular local figure due to his mastery of the Otomí Indian language and his encouragement of their learning useful arts and crafts. After Father Hidalgo's ordination in 1776, he briefly held responsible posts, including that of rector of *El Colegio de San Nicolás Obispo*, but his liberal ideas were unpopular with the hierarchy, whose wrath Hidalgo incurred in two separate attempts to improve the economic lot of his parishioners. Ignoring the fact that the Spanish crown forbade the making of wine or growing silkworms in the New World (to keep its domestic trade monopoly intact), Hidalgo imported grape vines on one occasion and mulberry trees on another, only to see them destroyed by royal soldiers and to face interrogation by the Spanish Inquisition.

By 1810 Hidalgo's main energies were devoted to conspiring for an uprising that he hoped would lead to Mexican independence. The center of the conspiracy was the city of Querétaro, some fifty miles southeast of Dolores on the road to Mexico City. His fellow conspirators, also *criollos*, planned to organize an insurrection and seize power from the *peninsulares* and their allies. While initially they would declare their fealty to King Ferdinand VII as a ruse, their clear final purpose was independence.

But royal authorities learned of the plot and arrested three of the conspirators, including the wife of a former governor of an Indian district (*corregidor*), who nevertheless was able to get a warning to Hidalgo. This woman, Doña Josefa Ortiz de Domínguez (*la Corregidora*), thereby achieved her own place in Mexican history.

Acting on the timely warning of *la Corregidora*, the three remaining principal actors in the revolt—Father Hidalgo and two royal cavalry officers, Capt. Ignacio Allende and Lieut. Juan Aldama—decided to move immediately, and for outright independence. The church bells were rung at Dolores early in the morning of September 16, 1810, and the assembled crowd of *mestizos* and *indios* heard a stirring address by Father Hidalgo, who called for the expulsion of the Spaniards and an end to bad governance and the burdensome system of Indian tribute to the Crown.

Propelled by Hidalgo's fiery *Grito de Dolores* ("cry of Dolores"), the ragtag army of 700

INDEPENDENCE: THE EARLY YEARS

During its first forty years of independence from Spain, Mexico reached its greatest territorial expansion. But the country also suffered through more than thirty presidencies and military *golpes*, to say nothing of the somewhat grotesque crowning of the Emperor of the Cactus Throne, Agustín I (formerly General Iturbide) on July 21, 1822, and *his* overthrow two years later. (Afterwards, Mexico became a republic, adopting a constitution based significantly on that of the U.S.)

began its march to nearby San Miguel, where it was reinforced by Captain Allende's cavalry. By the time it reached Celaya on its way toward its first major goal—the capture of the strategic provincial capital city of Guanajuato—the once-tiny revolutionary band had grown to 20,000.

Father Hidalgo's army arrived at Guanajuato on September 28 to find that the *peninsulares* and their supporters had retired to a well-constructed granary, which they had fortified. At first, royalist soldiers held off the rebels, who attacked in numbers and suffered many casualties. However, the heroism of a miner, who managed to set fire to the main gates of the granary and thus to permit the rebels' successful entry into the fortified building, allowed Hidalgo's forces to achieve victory.

Despite the exhortations of Hidalgo and Allende, the surrender of Guanajuato was followed by violence and pillage. The hated *encomenderos* and *hacendados* (landowners) were attacked and sometimes killed by the victorious peasants and miners, who had been exploited for decades. These excesses only redoubled the resolve of the viceroy in Mexico City to put down the rebellion. Hidalgo and his military commanders were excommunicated, and royalist forces were raised to march north and engage Hidalgo's troops. Meanwhile, Hidalgo's rebels had moved south to capture Valladolid and had defeated a small royalist force defending a strategic pass through the hills surrounding the Valley of Mexico.

The beginning of the end for Hidalgo came when, for reasons still not clear, he failed to take advantage of this opportunity to march on Mexico City and, by its capture, successfully to end the war for independence. Instead, perhaps not realizing the weakness of the royalists, he turned back, suffered a defeat at the hands of pursuing forces in Querétaro, and retreated to Guadalajara, where he was well received by the populace. Here he attempted to form a provisional government.

But a well-trained and -equipped royalist army was soon on the outskirts of Guadalajara. Though outnumbered by the rebels, the army soundly defeated them and forced Hidalgo and his principal lieutenants to flee toward sanctuary in the United States. On their way to the border, they were intercepted by royalist forces, captured, and condemned to death. After their execution in June 1811, their heads were hung on the corners of the granary in Guanajuato as a warning to those who opposed the King of Spain.

This period was marked not so much by problems with the United States or other foreign nations as by profound internal changes; a power struggle ensued between the established landowners who had survived the struggle for independence and reformist liberals with a modern vision of the state. Nevertheless, the confusion created by the collapse of the Spanish Empire and the emergence of an independent government resulted in weakness and ambiguity, and created an atmosphere of potential conflict between Mexico and its northern neighbor. Indeed, earlier U.S. dealings with the Spaniards, such as the Louisiana Purchase of 1803[1] and the Florida Purchase of 1819, had already begun a chain of events that in a few decades was to bring the two countries to war.

A major source of irritation was the boundary between Texas and Louisiana Territory. In 1812, the United States declared war on England and announced the annexation of Florida. This action raised questions about the territory lying between the U.S.'s Florida and Spain's Texas. It was already becoming apparent that the strength of the Spanish Empire was waning in the New World, and the United States was in a strong position to negotiate transcontinental frontiers. Finally, on February 22, 1819, a treaty was negotiated according to which the United States recognized Spanish sovereignty over territory that is now California, Arizona, New Mexico, and Texas in exchange for Spanish recognition of existing transcontinental boundaries. This Adams-Onis Treaty (or *Tratado Trascontinental* in Spanish) demonstrated the recognition by a major European state of the United States as a continent-wide power.

---

[1] The U.S. purchased Louisiana from France, which had acquired the territory from Spain in 1800. The vagueness of the boundaries of Louisiana covered by the purchase resulted in a serious dispute.

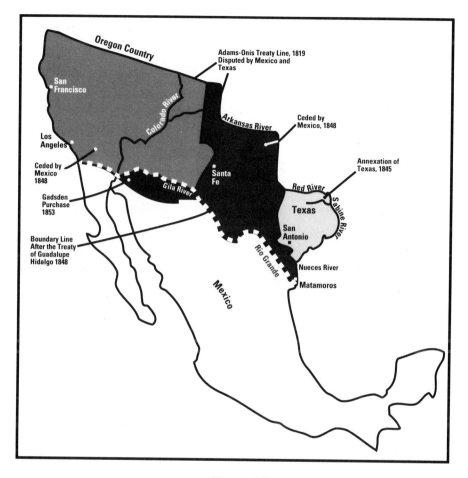

Figure 1.3
Significant changes in the U.S.-Mexico Border.

THE FIGHT FOR TEXAS

Relations between the United States and Mexico were initiated formally in February 1822 when Joel R. Poinsett of South Carolina was sent to Mexico as the first U.S. minister, followed a few months later by the appointment of José Manuel Zozaya as Mexico's minister to Washington.

Poinsett proved to be an able and observant diplomat. He

had learned Spanish through his sojourns to South America as an amateur botanist (our familiar Christmas flower, the poinsettia, is named after him). To his credit, Poinsett understood early that the most grave difficulty between the two young nations was the disposition of the unruly territory of Texas, which was already being settled by a few slaveholding emigrants from the Southern United States. These settlers seemed unlikely to be willing to live contentedly under Mexican laws, which required among other things an obligatory conversion to Catholicism and a "Spanish-language only" law for the conduct of all official business.

Poinsett was also shrewd enough to see the Mexican Empire of Agustín I as ephemeral in the face of republican sentiments and "imperial" inefficiency and greed, but the then-current Washington policy of encouraging New World colonies to declare their independence from Europe resulted in the premature recognition of the Mexican Empire on January 27, 1823, just two months before Iturbide abdicated and the Mexican Empire became a short-lived memory.

This same sentiment was manifested more dramatically several months later. On December 2, 1823, U.S. president James Monroe proclaimed what came to be known as the Monroe Doctrine, warning the European powers that further colonization—or, indeed, any form of intervention in the Americas—would be unacceptable to the United States. This policy remained effective during the following forty years, lapsing only when the United States became immersed in its Civil War.

Though brilliant, the Spanish-speaking Poinsett soon found himself more involved in Mexico's internal affairs than he should have been, and was accused by Mexicans of meddling. He was notably critical, in private at least, of Emperor Iturbide. Although the latter, a military strongman, was unpopular with his people, there was still resentment when the criticism came from an American diplomat.

Meddling aside, Poinsett was clearly more competent than his successor, Anthony Butler, who arrived on the scene early in 1830. Butler, a rude and sometimes violent man, was the antithesis of the courtly Poinsett. The new minister attempted to pressure Mexico to change the border to the United States's advantage (for example, it was proposed to move the border from the 42nd to the 37th parallel in the vicinity of the West Coast so as to include in U.S. territory the port city of San Francisco), in exchange for which Mexico was to receive a sum of money to be negotiated. Butler was also given instructions to inquire into a purchase price for Texas.

From 1825 until 1830 the situation in Mexico's northern area of Tejas-Coahuila, now known as Texas, had grown ever more volatile. A heavy inflow of American colonists—led by Robert Leftwich with 200 families, Hayden Edwards with 800 families, Green Dewitt with 300 families, and others—overwhelmed the Mexican settlers and the feeble Mexican military garrisons spread thinly throughout the immense and almost totally undeveloped area. All this was exacerbated by the slavery issue, one that a generation later was to play an important role in the American Civil War.

In any event, unrest was rampant in the 1820s, and a strong, local leadership was emerging. It was to the advantage of neither the emerging Texan leadership nor the beleaguered Mexican authorities when, in 1826, the maverick Hayden Edwards proclaimed from Nacogdoches the birth of the "Republic of Fredonia." Prompt joint action by a leading settler, Stephen Austin, and the local Mexican authorities soon put this rebellion down, and relations between the Mexican government and the Texans actually improved for a while. But this changed dramatically on September 15, 1829, when slavery was abolished throughout all the territory of Mexico—including, of course, what is now Texas. Colonists' resentment and restiveness caused the Mexican government to offer a carrot: All existing slaves could be maintained, but their children were free and no other slaves were to be allowed into Mexico in the future. However, the widespread evasion of this provision by the institution of phony work contracts as black slaves were brought in forced the Mexican government, in April 1830, to bar all further immigration from the United States, though Mexico continued to welcome European immigrants.

In response to the immigration ban, Austin, who had supported the Mexican authorities in the Fredonia case, organized a series of regional political conventions through 1831–32, which culminated in a decision to send Austin to Mexico City to petition for the establishment of Texas as a separate *estado* (state) within the Republic of Mexico. This would free the Texans from control by the neighboring state of Coahuila, whose governor had been given authority over them, and whose absentee rule (there is no record of a visit to Texas by a governor of Tejas-Coahuila), the Texans felt, had been capricious. The mission to the Mexican capital failed, and Austin was imprisoned for more than a year when a confidential report he was sending back to Texas was intercepted.

By the time he was released, Austin had come to believe that further accommodation with the ever-changing governance in Mexico City was impossible. (During this period the average tenure for a Mexican president was less than a year.) Accordingly, he began the discreet purchase of arms in preparation for the next fateful step: a fight for independence. While it is not surprising that the Anglo settlers in Texas proved eager to join his enterprise, it is remarkable that even many settlers who had their origins in Mexico favored independence from what they saw as the weak and vacillating government in Mexico City.

Before long, battles for Texas's independence were being fought under such leaders as William B. Travis, who seized Anáhuac (now Galveston) on June 30, 1835. This was followed in December by the surrender of San Antonio Bejar (now San Antonio). A formal declaration of independence was signed on March 1, 1836. There were setbacks, such as Mexican General Antonio López de Santa Anna's capture of San Antonio's Alamo just one week after the declaration was signed, a defeat marked by Santa Anna's summary execution of its defenders, including Davy Crockett and Jim Bowie. But the war for Texan independence ground inexorably on and was capped by the victory, at San Jacinto, of Texan troops led by Sam Houston over the Mexican army led by Santa Anna. The Mexican general (who was also serving one of his many presidential terms at the time) later recounted his surprise at not being executed after his surrender at San Jacinto, but Houston had other plans for him.

Under the duress of the moment, Santa Anna signed two agreements pledging him to withdraw his troops and to accept Texas's independence and its boundary at the Rio Grande (to Mexicans, *Rio Bravo y Grande del Norte)*, and, even more controversially, to attempt (unsuccessfully, it turns out) to persuade his government to abide by these accords. Santa Anna's capitulation brought him into temporary disrepute in Mexico, but he was later to rise again and again as a war hero and several-time president. Although Mexican government officials talked of reconquering Texas and never formally recognized its independence, internal weakness and lack of federal funds precluded any major military action.

Though forced by circumstances to this state, Mexicans were highly resentful of the loss of Texas and blamed the United States for the disaster, claiming that without the arms and other supplies pouring in from the U.S., the Texans could not have prosecuted the war for independence so successfully. Adding insult to injury, in December 1845 the U.S. Congress formally annexed Texas, making it the 28th state in the Union. This prompted Mexico to sever diplomatic relations with the U.S. for a period.

THE WAR OF THE NORTH AMERICAN INVASION

In the view of many Mexican historians, the secession of Texas from Mexico and its subsequent annexation by the U.S. were only the first of a series of calculated steps that led in 1846 to what Mexicans call "The War of the North American Invasion" and Americans call "The Mexican War." This war had its roots in what the American journalist John L. O'Sullivan, in the December 1845 issue of the *Democratic Review,* called "the right of our Manifest Destiny to overspread and to possess the whole continent, which Providence has given us for the development of the great experiment of Liberty." It was not long in coming.

It is clear in retrospect that by the autumn of 1845, when American president James Polk sent special envoy John Slidell to Mexico, Polk was already prepared to initiate hostilities. Polk must have anticipated that Slidell's offer to purchase what is now western Texas, New Mexico, Arizona, and California for $30 million would be seen as totally unacceptable to the Mexicans. Indeed, the Mexicans had on principle rejected many times in the past the sale of Mexican territory at any price. Even had this not been the case, internal problems in Mexico, including yet another *coup d'état,* would have prevented any formal response to Slidell's offer at the time it was presented. On January 13, 1846, at a time when a new and inexperienced Mexican government was still refusing to meet with Slidell and claiming that Mexican territory included all of Texas, President Polk issued orders to Gen. Zachary Taylor to establish a military presence along the Rio Grande.

By mid-April, the construction of Ft. Brown, across the river from the Mexican city of Matamoros, had been undertaken. The U.S. presence was burgeoning. The "War of the North American Invasion" began on April 25, 1846, when a Mexican cavalry unit crossed the river and fired on a patrol of U.S. soldiers on the banks of the Rio Grande. Eleven Yankees were killed, six

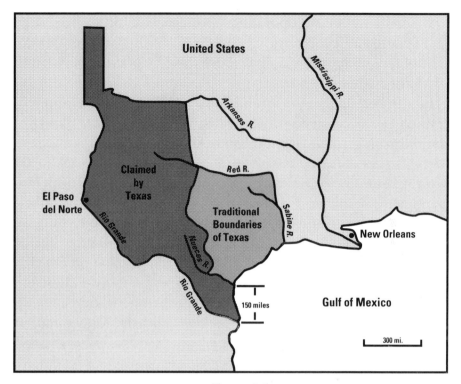

Figure 1.4
The U.S.-Texas Border Dispute.

wounded, and 63 taken prisoner. General Taylor promptly announced that "hostilities may now be considered as commenced," and, with a U.S. Army cavalry force soon augmented by several regiments of Texan and Louisiana volunteers, moved slowly and deliberately south to capture Monterrey, the regional capital of the state of Nuevo León.

Meanwhile, a battle plan executed by Gen. Winfield Scott, the commander-in-chief of U.S. forces, was underway on several fronts. Gen. Stephen Kearny's forces in Missouri marched on Santa Fe, captured it, proceeded through Arizona, and engaged Mexican forces defending California. The U.S. Pacific fleet under Commodore John D. Sloat was ordered to seize San Francisco and Monterey. These operations were successfully completed, and California secured, in January 1847. In the Gulf of Mexico, U.S. Navy units under Commodore David Conner successfully blockaded Mexican ports.

Not surprisingly, the multi-front attack by well-equipped, trained U.S. forces caused great dismay and political unrest in the Mexican capital. General Santa Anna, once again recalled to serve as president and commander-in-chief, found himself faced with substantial American armies in the north and south, his ports blockaded, and a much-divided Mexican body politic throughout the country. For example, an ill-advised effort by Santa Anna's predecessors to finance the war by seizing Church property and possessions caused a massive reaction on the part of many conservative, influential Mexicans, to say nothing of the powerful clergy. Even though the government soon gave up this tactic, much resentment remained, and the long-standing division between the clergy and landowners on the one hand and reformist liberals on the other was even more exacerbated.

As the war progressed with a series of U.S. victories, Santa Anna was wise and courageous enough to realize that further resistance to the American forces would only cause greater suffering for his people. Thus, his government entered into negotiations with Nicholas P. Trist, a personal representative sent by President Polk. But these negotiations were soon stalemated, in part by the intransigence of Mexicans who did not share Santa Anna's views, and the campaign began anew. After a bloody struggle, General Scott captured Mexico City on September 14, 1847, effectively bringing the Mexican War to a conclusion. Although many brave young soldiers on both sides were lost in the fighting, the campaign for Mexico City is best remembered by Mexicans today for the heroic defense of historic Chapultepec Castle, located on a strategic high point with a commanding view of the city. The castle was defended by nine hundred soldiers and 47 heroic cadets of the military college located there.

Four of the teenaged cadets were wounded, 37 were taken prisoner, and six died in the battle. Annual ceremonies still mark the event in Chapultepec Park, where a monument to *Los Niños Héroes* has been erected.

Following General Scott's victory in Mexico City, several months of arduous negotiations between the two countries led to the signing, on February 2, 1848, of the Treaty of Guadalupe Hidalgo. Under the terms of the treaty, ratified by both governments at the end of May 1848, Mexico gave up all claims to Texas and ceded New Mexico, Arizona, and California—virtually all its territory north of the Rio Grande—to the United States. In return for the cession of more than half its territory, Mexico received a cash payment of $15 million and relief from all outstanding claims by U.S. citizens, such claims to be considered and paid by the U.S. government.

But Scott's victory brought more than huge territorial gains to the United States. The siege of Chapultepec and the death of *los niños héroes*, which have epitomized the "War of the North American Invasion" to generations of Mexicans, created in Mexico a degree of hatred, humiliation, and xenophobia—particularly anti-Americanism—that remained strong for generations, and has never fully dissipated. The failure of Americans today to understand the legacy of the Mexican War—indeed, most Americans seem unacquainted even with its broad outlines—stands as a barrier to the awareness of Mexican sensitivities so vital to a healthy relationship between the neighboring countries.

The sad end of the affair did not play out until 1853, when Santa Anna, serving as Mexico's president for the eleventh time in his long and stormy career, and much in need of ready cash, agreed to the Gadsden Purchase. He thus raised $10 million by the sale of 30,000 square miles of territory in what is now southern New Mexico and southeastern Arizona. This so sickened the Mexican people that they rose against Santa Anna, who went into his final exile, never to reappear on the scene.

THE PRESIDENCY OF BENITO JUÁREZ: A NEW ERA BEGINS

A group of liberal thinkers emerged after Santa Anna's down-fall late in 1853. Headed by an old rebel leader, Juan Alvarez, as the provisional president succeeding Santa Anna, they called for a Constitutional Convention to establish a liberal, demo-cratic government, and the beginning of a new era of gover-nance in Mexico. In the summer of 1855, President Alvarez embarked on a period of government restructuring called *la Reforma*, which among other things abolished *fueros*, an old privilege of Spanish origin that had long exempted members of the military and the clergy from trial by civilian courts. Up to now, neither military courts martial nor clerical hearings often resulted in justice being done in the cases of military men or members of the clergy accused of common crimes. According to *la Reforma*, however, they were henceforth to be tried by civilian courts.

In the aftermath of the humiliating lost war with the United States, Mexico was fortunate to be able to turn for leadership to one of her finest historical figures—Benito Juárez, a full-blooded Zapotec Indian who rose from humble beginnings to serve as a liberal governor of Oaxaca in 1848. By 1855, Juárez, who had been exiled to New Orleans by Santa Anna, was back as private secretary to the provisional president, Juan Alvarez, and was one of a new triumvirate of liberal leaders of the country, along with Melchor Ocampo, the liberal governor of Michoacán and a philosopher with European leanings, and Santos Degollado, a general in the revolt that overthrew Santa Anna for the last time and, later, governor of Jalisco.

When President Juárez took office, he was faced with numerous problems caused by *la Guerra de la Reforma* (the War of the Reform, 1858–61): inflation, abrasive social frictions, wide-spread destruction of infrastructure, and a steep drop in agricul-tural and industrial production. In an effort to ameliorate these pressing problems, Juárez suspended all payments on Mexico's foreign debt.

Unfortunately, this action, misunderstood to some extent, met with a powerful, immediate, and negative reaction from the European powers, who quickly condemned the Mexican president. Much to their later chagrin, England and Spain joined with France in organizing a jointly manned fleet with troops on board and orders to capture Mexican ports and to exact payment of the foreign debt.

While England and Spain wished only to seize customs payments and to pressure Juárez into paying off Mexico's debt, France, under Emperor Napoleon III, had something more sinister in mind—a new conquest of Mexico, and its rule by a European "emperor" of his choosing. Despite the protestations of the governments of Queen Victoria and Queen Isabella II, the French emperor persisted, eventually precipitating the withdrawal of English and Spanish troops. This left the French free to carry out their dramatic and far-reaching plan of armed intervention.

EARLY MEXICAN VICTORY AT PUEBLA: THE "CINCO DE MAYO"

Shortly thereafter, some 6,500 French troops under the veteran Gen. Charles Ferdinand Latrille de Lorencz marched from the port of Veracruz to take the old colonial city of Puebla, thought to be filled with conservative sympathizers. But President Juárez had other plans. He sent a capable Mexican general, Ignacio Zaragoza, and some 2,000 veteran troops to defend the city. The Mexicans acquitted themselves well. On May 5, 1862, a frenzied French attack ordered by General Lorencz was beaten off. Having sustained heavy casualties, the invaders retreated to Orizaba, leaving the Mexicans with a day still celebrated wherever they may gather—the Cinco de Mayo.

Alas, this famous victory proved to be ephemeral. Napoleon

III, hearing of the humbling defeat, ordered 30,000 reinforcements to sail immediately to Mexico and to overwhelm the Juárez government, still weak from the devastation of the War of the Reform and under attack from within by conservative clergy, the landed gentry, and pro-French monarchists. The French force, several times larger in size than before, surrounded Puebla and bombarded it into submission, meanwhile sending special forces to interdict the Mexico City–Puebla railways and prevent Juárez from sending supplies to his beleaguered city. Once Puebla fell, in May 1863, the French army encountered little resistance on its march to Mexico City.

Initially determined to defend Mexico City, Juárez was convinced by his military advisers that it would be wiser to abandon the city to the French army and set up a new capital in remote and more easily defended San Luis Potosí. The French army entered Mexico City on June 10, 1863, to the cheers of the conservatives, and a Te Deum was offered in their honor in Mexico City's magnificent Cathedral.

THE UNHAPPY REIGN OF EMPEROR MAXIMILIAN

Shortly thereafter, Napoleon III and his conservative Mexican allies called on the young Archduke Ferdinand Maximilian of Hapsburg to serve as emperor of Mexico. The Mexicans who paid the Austrian archduke a visit in his Adriatic palace assured him that there was a groundswell of popular fervor in Mexico for him to become emperor, and he agreed to do so. It was not long before he and his tall, beautiful, young wife Charlotte (Carlota, to the Mexicans) were sailing to Mexico.

Mexican Church leaders and other conservatives were delighted at the arrival of the new rulers. They fully anticipated that Maximilian would move quickly in their support—for example, to annul the laws of *la Reforma* and to return Church property confiscated by previous liberal governments. But the

Figure 1.5
Maximilian and Carlota.

new emperor had other thoughts; himself a member of the Masonic order, and hoping to gain favor with the liberals, he did not think it wise to permit the arch-conservative Church to regain its old property and perquisites. Not only spurning the entreaties of a Papal Nuncio recently arrived from Rome, he actually pressed the Church for some emergency loans to help meet the expenses of his new government.

The fact that the emperor was holding the Church and its allies at arms length, however, did little to mollify the liberals, who had been driven from Mexico City by French troops. Juárez, whose Republican government had been recognized *de jure* by U.S. president Abraham Lincoln, moved his capital north from San Luis Potosí to Chihuahua, and, finally to El Paso del Norte (Ciudad Juárez today) as pressures from French troops grew.

Lincoln's support of Juárez was necessarily tempered by the exigencies of the American Civil War. For one thing, military assistance for Juárez and his beleaguered Republican army was impractical at a time when Union forces were stretched thin. For another, Lincoln—who might otherwise have overtly supported the Mexican Republicans—did not want to risk an angry Napoleon III intervening on the side of the Confederacy. Thus, during the 1861–64 period America's hands were more or less tied.

But the year 1865 was to prove fateful for Maximilian. On the domestic front, lulled by his army's apparent successes against the Republicans, and acting on a false rumor that Juárez had fled to the United States, he signed on October 3 the infamous *Decreto de la Bandera Negra* (Black Flag Decree), which called for the summary execution within twenty-four hours of anyone caught bearing arms and opposing his regime, including "all persons belonging to armed bands or corps, not legally authorized." Thousands of Mexican soldiers captured while fighting honorably for the Republic were executed under the terms of this terrible imperial decree, which ignited a deep surge of opposition to the French-imposed emperor and a renewed dedication to his overthrow.

The Union victory in the American Civil War in 1865 was another blow to Maximilian. No longer concerned about French reaction, and influenced by the likes of Secretary of State William Seward and Gen. U.S. Grant, the U.S. administration felt free to encourage Juárez and to support the Republican cause more openly. Thousands of tons of surplus war materials, purchased on credit by Juárez, were soon finding their way through circuitous routes to the Republican army. Accustomed to battle and lured by good salaries, about three thousand Union veterans of the American Civil War joined the Republican army and fought side by side with the troops of Benito Juárez against Emperor Maximilian. But the Emperor had, in turn, recruited some two thousand mostly Confederate veterans to fight on his side!

Meanwhile, Empress Carlota, sensing that the tide was turning against her husband's government and burdened with news that French support was weakening, returned to Europe to plead her husband's cause with Napoleon III and the Pope. Not only did both the French court and the Vatican ignore her pleas (the Pope wondered aloud why Maximilian had not returned Church lands and properties), but a group of courtiers and Papal advisers decided that she was suffering from a mental illness. Thus the Empress Marie Charlotte Amelie, daughter of the king and queen of Belgium and cousin of Queen Victoria, was confined to a Belgian home, where—judged to be insane—she lived on for sixty long and tragic years.

Nothing went well for Maximilian after Carlota's departure. Spurred on by a new flow of U.S. support and by the vacillating policies of Napoleon III, the implacable man who had sworn to overcome Maximilian—Benito Juárez—resumed the offensive early in 1866. By the year's end, Republican generals had captured such strategic sites as Monterrey, Tampico, Guaymas, Guadalajara, and Juarez's birthplace, Oaxaca.

The Mexican emperor, heartsick about the French perfidy (Napoleon III was withdrawing his troops and urging Maximilian's abdication, to which the proud Hapsburg would not agree) and Carlota's confinement in Belgium, courageously made a final and clandestine journey to the north to take personal command of the last contingent of the Imperial army, which was holding out in the city of Querétaro. Shortly after his arrival there, the Imperial garrison was completely encircled by a much larger force of Republican troops and the emperor was faced with the choice of either surrendering or attempting to flee alone through enemy lines and desert his remaining troops. On May 15, 1867, Maximilian turned over his sword to the Republican general Mariano Escobedo.

Despite worldwide appeals that Maximilian be spared, the military tribunal convened to hear his case convicted him of capital crimes, including the issuance of the infamous Black Flag Decree. The death sentence, approved by President Juárez, was carried out by firing squad on June 19, 1867.

MEXICO ENTERS THE MODERN AGE

On July 15, 1867, in stark and deliberate contrast to the gilded carriages and pomp that had marked the entourage of the emperor, Benito Juárez arrived in Mexico City in the simple, black carriage that had carried him through years of struggle against the French intervention.[2] Juárez wasted little time on the triumphal ceremonies greeting the restoration of the Republic. He soon announced his candidacy for an unprecedented third term as president (his first two terms had been largely spent in the struggle against the French). He was easily re-elected, and on December 1, 1867, was sworn in to the presidential office for the third time.

---

[2] This carriage may now be seen in a place of honor at Chapultepec Castle.

The government of the newly restored Republic was faced with an immense economic and social challenge. The rebuilding job after years of French intervention and war was heroic. Juárez named Matías Romero—who, as Juárez's official representative in Washington during the early 1860s, had been instrumental in gaining U.S. support for the liberation of Mexico—to the most important cabinet position, minister of finance. Romero, a skilled economic planner, shortly announced a program to improve Mexican infrastructure (highways, railroads, dams, potable water projects) and the development of industry, agriculture, and natural resources—particularly mining, to which he gave a special priority. Romero sought and obtained considerable foreign credits and began to look for foreign private direct investment for these projects.

Private investors were nervous about the stability and safety of their proposed projects in Mexico, particularly in the countryside. However, the creation of the *rurales* (federal rural police who enforced law and order in the countryside), as well as the credibility of Romero and his economic team, did much to allay these fears; by the late 1860s foreign investors were traveling all over Mexico in search of mining and other opportunities.

THE PORFIRIATO: 1876–1910

Mexico was desolated in mid-July 1872, when the popular President Juárez died suddenly of a heart attack. Although his successor, Sebastián Lerdo de Tejada (who was subsequently elected president in his own right in October 1872) continued Juárez's policies, the new president was less effective and more vulnerable to the growing opposition led by Gen. Porfirio Díaz, a war hero who had served brilliantly as a cavalry commander at the Battle of Puebla and had subsequently risen rapidly through the officer corps.

President Lerdo de Tejada, though he was widely admired,

had neither the charisma nor the military support of General Díaz. So when, in mid-1876, Díaz launched a revolt, he had little difficulty in prevailing against the forces of Lerdo de Tejada. Díaz occupied Mexico City on November 21, allowing his adversary safe conduct to Veracruz and a steamship waiting to carry him into exile in the United States.

Porfirio Díaz began his 34-year (direct and indirect) reign by drawing heavily on plans for economic stability and social development undertaken successfully by his two predecessors, Juárez and Lerdo de Tejada. The years of *la Reforma* had laid a solid groundwork for economic growth and development. Díaz, wishing for a dramatic increase in foreign investment and American good will in general, quickly came to an agreement on some long-standing claims by U.S. citizens and paid off more than $4 million during 1877 alone. As conditions began to stabilize in Mexico, Díaz called for elections, winning a four-year presidential term with ease.

Following his election, Díaz continued to work to improve United States–Mexico relations. One of his first moves was to hold a series of meetings with American officials on such border problems as marauding *bandidos* who would attack settlements and steal cattle on the U.S. side of the border. He established a mechanism for inviting visiting U.S. traders and investors to Mexico, and had new legislation passed that improved the investment climate. He also opened three new Mexican consulates along the border (at El Paso, Laredo, and Eagle Pass) to stimulate trade and investment.

Favorably impressed by the new regime, American president Rutherford B. Hayes recognized the Díaz government in the spring of 1877. Investment and trade began slowly to build, and U.S. and European investment soon emerged as a principal engine of growth in the Mexican economy; for example, in mining, petroleum, agriculture, and industry.

Mexico's new leader was faced with a political dilemma in

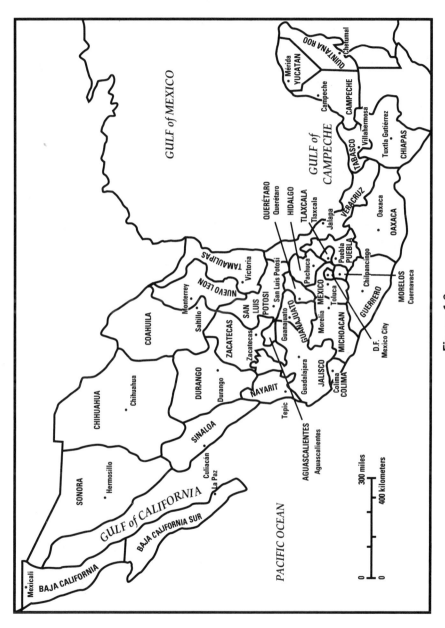

Figure 1.6
Historic Cities of Mexico.

1880. He had scored his initial triumph in part on the basis of the slogan of *no-reelección* (literally, no re-election—but interpreted by Díaz as meaning no consecutive re-election!). Thus, to honor his commitment, he needed, and soon discovered, a suitable stand-in to run for the presidency while Díaz managed affairs from behind the scenes. His candidate was Gen. Manuel González, who served nominally as president from 1880–84 in a term marked by petty scandals. Needless to say, Don Porfirio had no difficulty in presenting himself for the presidency in 1884, and, as *el Indispensable*, easily winning back the office.

Díaz is often misundertood as a sycophant playing for the favor of U.S. and other foreign governments and investors. In fact—an interesting paradox—he saw the opening of the Mexican economy to international trade and investment as a way to strengthen the country against undue foreign influence. Under the positivist rubric of *orden y progreso* (order and progress) Díaz began the immense task of building modern Mexico. Indeed, despite all the criticism that has been leveled at his regime, Diaz's first decades in office were marked by extensive economic development. A huge array of tasks was attacked within the period of a few years: Thousands of new factories were built, creating substantial employment. Mail service was greatly improved, and the mining industry modernized. Modern agricultural methods were introduced; the railway system was extended and upgraded; telegraph lines and dock facilities were built. Public education and health care were expanded and brought up to date.

Díaz also played his political hand well. While a convinced liberal, he was able to come to a satisfactory accommodation with the Church, in part by allowing it to hold on to and even modestly expand its properties, including the establishment of new convents and seminaries. As soon as he felt more secure politically, he had the *no-reelección* provisions of the law rescinded, so that he no longer had to rely on straw men in his exercise of power.

The Mexican economy began to boom under Díaz, who was able to pay off the foreign debt by 1890 and to balance the federal budget by 1894, even generating a slight surplus. U.S. and British oil companies established a profitable oil industry, which paid taxes into the Mexican government coffers. By 1908 a huge railway crisscrossed Mexico, and Mexican reserves had risen to the huge sum (in those days) of 70 million gold pesos. More than 3,000 mines—840 of them foreign, mostly American—were producing silver, gold, copper, zinc, iron, and lead, making Mexico one of the world's top producers. Electrical plants were built; electric lights and streetcars became common in Mexico's major cities.

This economic growth was highly asymmetrical. Urban dwellers and the middle and upper classes were the principal recipients, while the rural population outside the modern agricultural sector was virtually unaffected by the progress. Nevertheless, by 1910 Mexico represented a respectable, emerging economy.

2 THE COSMIC RACE (1910–24)

Debate continues in Mexico to this day about the role of Porfirio Díaz in Mexico's development. Was he a helpful force in Mexico's modernization, acting in the best interests of his country? Or was he, as held by some historians, a simple doormat for foreign capitalists?

In the judgment of Daniel Cosío Villegas, Mexico's foremost historian, Don Porfirio for all his faults was no lackey; he acted in what he believed to be the need for his country to enter the 20th century as a modern, industrial nation. During the boom period of the *porfiriato* (1876–1910), an astounding $2 billion in foreign private direct investment—half of it American—was attracted to Mexico. These investments, involving thousands of U.S. and Mexican firms and individuals and encompassing the widest range of commercial interests, speeded the growth of economic and social interdependence between the United States and Mexico.

By 1909, when William Howard Taft became the first U.S. president to visit Mexico, this billion-dollar U.S. investment in Mexican enterprises had spread from oil and gas, railroads, mines, and textiles to service industries such as insurance companies and banks. Similar amounts of funds had come in from Europe—chiefly Great Britain, Germany, and France. The Mexican economy had grown robust and internationally respected.

Díaz had inherited a country with 640 kilometers of railway track and left it with 20,000 kilometers extending throughout the country—although, as critics remarked, rail lines were planned by foreign engineers and tended to connect industrial and mining centers and ignore the needs of the countryside. To limit the rapidly growing influence of British and U.S. interests in the transportation industry, Jose I. Limantour, a brilliant treasury secretary, created the *Ferrocarriles Nacionales de México*, the national railroad company, and, by an adroit combination of persuasion and veiled warnings, obtained a part interest in foreign investments in the railway sector. During the *porfiriato*, huge strides in mining production also made Mexico a leading world exporter of silver, copper, and other metals and minerals.

But there is a darker side to the *porfiriato*, which contributed heavily to its eventual downfall. Díaz and his followers, recall, had adopted the positivist credo, *orden y progreso* (order and progress). Of these two objectives, Díaz—a career military officer and a hero of the Battle of Puebla—stressed the former. He used the iron hand of his military and the dreaded *rurales*, or paramilitary national police, to keep peace in factories and in the countryside. These forces could be counted on to side with landowners and industrialists threatened with labor dissent, which was kept to a minimum during the long years of the *porfiriato*; they were the backbone of Díaz's "generation of peace."

Thus, in the rural Mexico of Porfirio Díaz, some 800 *hacendados* controlled more than 90 percent of arable land and exploited some 5 million landless peasants on their vast farms and ranches. Taking into account the complex payment arrangement for the *peones*—and the custom of deducting food and other "expenses" from their pay before they received it—it has been estimated that their actual salary was about thirty cents per day.

Conditions were not much better in Mexico's rapidly expanding industrial sector. Factory workers typically were employed for six 12-hour shifts per week, and earned about $7 per week. Safety conditions were poor, and industrial accidents and deaths were common. Even so, the wage differential between the rural and urban industrial sectors was enough to create a steady flow of internal migration from the land to the cities that would continue, though at a decreasing rate, until the present time. This, in turn, has provided Mexican industry over the decades with an excess supply of workers, permitting rapid industrial growth while keeping wages down to a historical level of about one-tenth of equivalent U.S. wages.

Withal, one-half of Mexico's population, including indigenous peoples in remote areas, lived throughout the *porfiriato* very much as they had for a thousand years, largely unaffected by the economic boom of 1880–1910. But for those privileged to enjoy it, the *porfiriato* was a time of cultural growth in literature, poetry, and the arts. The architecture of the period was typically eclectic, with liberal borrowings from French and Italian styles. When the *Palacio de Bellas Artes* was built in the early years of the new century, its mammoth stage was adorned by a twenty-ton glass curtain designed in the United States by Louis Tiffany, along with an elaborate steel mechanism to open and close it.[1]

To foreign investors, Díaz was a godsend: He paid off the

---

[1] This curtain, still in daily use, has been seen by millions of American and other tourists who have visited the Palace of Fine Arts to see the famous Ballet Folklórico.

national debt in full, created a national bank that could deal efficiently with foreign investors and traders, and offered internal order to foreign businessmen interested in Mexican investment and trade opportunities.

But in stark contrast to the rosy international economic situation, which enriched a narrow few at the top of Mexico's elite (the Catholic Church also profited immensely from its privileged position during the *porfiriato*) stood the hatred of the regime by a growing number of intellectuals, workers, and peasants led by such revolutionary heroes as the Flores Magón brothers. Even after their organization of strikes and demonstrations in Mexico had led to their exile to the United States, the brothers continued to publish their radical workers' newspaper, *Regeneración*—for which, at the insistence of the Mexican government, they were charged and convicted with violation of U.S. neutrality laws and imprisoned for three years in Arizona.

As early as 1906, the activities of the Flores Magón group and a critical number of other labor organizers and agitators were starting to weaken the industrial base of the *porfiriato*. More than four hundred strikes and other labor actions in Mexican industries and mines between 1906 and 1910 heralded the beginning of the end for the old regime. The situation was exacerbated by an ill-advised interview the aging dictator gave to an American journalist, James Creelman. In the interview, Díaz indicated that, after 34 years on the stage or in the wings of power, he would not seek re-election in the 1910 presidential race. This "announcement," which Díaz later tried unsuccessfully to retract, stirred up the opposition at a time when unrest in the urban industrial and rural areas was peaking.

Quick to take advantage of the uncertain situation was a greatly respected Mexican aristocrat from the north.

A series of statements on the Mexican presidential succession of 1910 issued by Francisco I. Madero, a wealthy landowner of pronounced liberal political views, captured great popular at-

Figure 2.1
Francisco I. Madero.

tention and support all over the country. Although Madero did not explicitly call for Díaz's overthrow (he suggested that Díaz, as an elder statesman and patriot, should see the advantages of voluntary retirement!), his writings and speeches converted Madero quickly into a national hero. In 1910 Madero was chosen as the presidential candidate of a number of opposition parties, including one calling for a single presidential term with no possibility of re-election for the lifetime of the incumbent.

Madero's meteoric rise to popularity—he toured Mexico in his election campaign train, speaking to audiences measured in the tens of thousands—did not go unnoticed by the Díaz authorities, who had him arrested in June 1910 and imprisoned on trumped-up charges of "fomenting rebellion and insulting the President of the Republic." In subsequent weeks several thousand of Madero's party workers also were imprisoned, and hundreds of thousands of supporters were discouraged by intimidation from appearing on election day. Madero was released on bail and ordered to remain in San Luis Potosí. In late September, however, he jumped bail and escaped to Laredo, Texas.

After the election, officials declared that Porfirio Díaz had been almost unanimously re-elected President, with Madero receiving only 196 votes! This was neither the first nor the last time that election figures have been juggled in Mexico, but is certainly the most laughable. As the dapper Madero himself put it when informed of the results, "Why, I have more relatives than that who voted for me!"

In the event, a combination of flagrant electoral fraud, labor unrest centered in the mining and textile industries, and the 80-year-old Díaz's clear determination to stay in power indefinitely finally overcame Madero's reservations about leading a movement for the overthrow, by force if necessary, of the senescent—and by this time, embarrassing—Don Porfirio. Working closely with collaborators around the country, Madero, from his self-imposed exile in the U.S., declared that "the violent and illegal system [of Porfirio Díaz] can no longer exist" and designated 6 p.m. on November 20, 1910, as the precise moment for "all the towns in the republic to rise in arms." The response to Madero's call was in some cases ill-timed, causing a number of early rebels to be massacred by federal troops. Nevertheless, the uprising soon became nationwide and inexorable. The rebellion's first success, in the northern border state of Chihuahua, was followed by victories in a number of other states throughout Mexico. The capture of Ciudad Juárez (in Chihuahua, across the Rio Grande from El Paso, Texas), a key center for U.S.-Mexico trade, contributed greatly to the rebels's domination of northern Mexico. High-spirited American supporters of the Revolution lined the banks of the river to follow the action and greet the federal forces' defeat with cheers.

As President Díaz quickly and decisively lost control of northern Mexico to the insurgents, he came to the realization that the long era of the *porfiriato* was coming to an end. On May 21, 1911, his representatives met secretly with Madero in Ciudad Juárez and agreed that Díaz would leave office within thirty days. In fact, before that month had passed, the old dictator had boarded a waiting ship and sailed off to France for a golden exile. One of his final remarks was a telling one: "Madero has unleashed a tiger, now let us see if he can control it!"

THE SHORT, SAD TERM OF FRANCISCO I. MADERO

With Díaz's departure, Madero made a triumphal journey from Chihuahua to Mexico City, where he was greeted by multitudes of admirers, including his ally from the south, the charismatic Emiliano Zapata. But Zapata's admiration soon turned to hatred when Madero proved unable or unwilling to meet Zapata's demands for the immediate distribution of land to his peasant supporters. When federal forces subsequently fired on *zapatistas* who had disarmed at Madero's request, this hostility became irreversible.

The vastly different ideologies of these two heroes, Madero and Zapata, symbolize the tragedy of the Revolution: Madero, a political liberal but economic conservative from the north, believed in bringing democratic government to a nation that respected private-property rights; Zapata, an indigenous leader of the south, believed in a Revolution that would eliminate large landholdings and redistribute land to the peasants.

The conflict between Madero and Zapata was only one of innumerable problems that soon caused the major leaders of the Mexican Revolution to be at each other's throats at one time or another throughout the course of the next decade (1910–20). While between one and two million Mexicans were dying on the battlefields, internecine warfare among revolutionary factions wreaked havoc on the Mexican economy and ripped the social fabric to shreds.

On a number of occasions during the tragic military phase of the Revolution, it looked like peace was at hand. The first of these was when the popular Madero and José María Pino Suárez were sworn in as president and vice-president, respectively, of Mexico early in November 1911. It soon became apparent to everyone, however, that Madero was more interested in political than in economic reform. Indeed, his family and friends, all *hacendados* in northern Mexico, had no intention of turning their lands over to the peasants. But for many rebels, ¡*Pan y tierra!*— Bread and land!—was the rallying cry. Led by Zapata, a number of leaders, including the northern hero Pancho Villa, were soon in arms against the new Madero regime.

It was not the rebels in the field, but internal treachery, however, that cost Madero his presidential sash—and his life. A revolt was organized within the army; Madero unwisely named Gen. Victoriano Huerta to put it down. For decades, Huerta had been a loyal follower of Porfirio Díaz.

For ten days in February 1913 (*la Decena Trágica*), artillery fire and military sorties inflicted great damage and uncounted civilian casualties throughout Mexico City. (Contemporary accounts tell of thousands of bloated bodies rotting in the streets, with people too fearful of the deadly crossfire to attempt to collect them.) The treacherous General Huerta took advantage of the confusion and terror to come to an agreement with the military officers opposing Madero and stage a *coup* of his own. He ordered Madero arrested. Within days the former President been "shot while trying to escape"—a story virtually no one believed.

The U.S. ambassador to Mexico at the time, Henry Lane Wilson, bears at least some moral responsibility for this outrage, and few Mexicans have forgotten this, creating a burden for American diplomats in Mexico that lasts to this day. During the course of a meeting at the U.S. Embassy that Ambassador Wilson had arranged, General Huerta and the counter-revolutionary leader Félix Díaz (a nephew of the exiled Don Porfirio) jointly agreed to the overthrow of the legitimate government of President Madero and its replacement by a government to be headed by Huerta. While there is no convincing evidence that Wilson specifically condoned Madero's death, neither is there any doubt that he wanted Madero replaced with someone more amenable to foreign interests. In any case, Madero's murder was a senseless act, which, alas, was a prototype of the countless tragedies that marked the next dark years of Mexico's history.

THE HUERTA REGIME AND WOODROW WILSON

Once installed as president, Huerta not surprisingly began a reign of terror: the assassination of political opponents, involuntary conscription into a federal army that was quintupled in size, and the accommodation of former military and civilian followers of the exiled Porfirio Díaz, many of them Huerta's longtime personal friends.

Huerta was soon involved in full-scale battles against a range of opponents whose names are still famous in Mexico: Villa, Zapata, Venustiano Carranza, Alvaro Obregón, and many others who saw Huerta as a betrayer of the ideals of the Revolution. Fortunately for Huerta, though, these insurgent leaders were often fighting each other as well.

Huerta was most anxious to gain, for his regime of questionable legitimacy, the formal recognition of the United States government. Despite the U.S. ambassador's recommendations, President Taft, in his waning days in office, decided to defer a decision on recognition to his successor. The idealistic new president, Woodrow Wilson (no relation to the ambassador), who like many Americans had been shocked by the news of Madero's assassination and thousands of reported casualties, refused to do so unless Huerta agreed to a general cease-fire and free elections in which Huerta would not be a candidate. Needless to say, Huerta refused this proposal. The civil war in Mexico continued, leaving the newly inaugurated President Wilson and his secretary of state, William Jennings Bryan, to devise new policies for dealing with insurgent Mexico. Shortly afterward Ambassador Wilson was recalled under a cloud. The Wilson administration's opposition to the Huerta regime was growing clear.

Initially, demonstrations of U.S. unhappiness with Huerta were confined to sending military equipment and other supplies to the northern insurgents including Carranza and Villa; but when that had no immediate result, Wilson decided upon a course of direct military intervention. Early in 1914 the U.S. naval and marine forces in the Gulf of Mexico were substantially reinforced. Shortly thereafter an "incident" occurred that was to precipitate the direct U.S. action the president had anticipated.

THE *DOLPHIN* INCIDENT

In April 1914, crew members of *USS Dolphin*, dispatched to the port city of Tampico, Mexico, to seek needed motor fuel for the ship's boats, were arrested by Huerta's coast guard when they arrived at a "restricted" fueling dock. Though the sailors were soon released, tempers had so flared on both sides that when, a few days later, the U.S. consul in Veracruz reported that a German ship bearing arms for Huerta's forces would soon arrive at that major port, the atmosphere was right for a sharp American reaction.

President Wilson immediately ordered the occupation by U.S. Marines of Veracruz, which was easily accomplished by the substantial U.S. forces in the area—but at the cost of a number of Mexican military and civilian casualties and considerable outcry throughout Mexico. The American consulate general in Monterrey was attacked, and the flag burned. Reports reached Washington that another U.S. flag had been tied to the tail of a donkey and used to clean the streets of Mexico City.

The impact of these reports upon Washington can well be imagined. The marine and navy contingent in Veracruz was substantially strengthened; rumors that United States military forces would soon march on Mexico City were not denied (though such a move was never anticipated). Huerta thus found himself impelled to withdraw considerable forces from the battles being waged against Carranza, Obregón, and Villa and assign them to defend the capital. Meanwhile, Wilson's generous supply of military and other material to the Mexican insurgents was beginning to take its toll on Huerta's depleted forces, resulting notably in Villa's capture of Zacatecas in northern Mexico and further actions by an emboldened Zapata in the south.

Huerta soon recognized that the situation that had befallen him was due in no small part to the actions of the man he called *"el puritano en la Casa Blanca"* (the Puritan in the White House). It is true that President Wilson quite deliberately tried to orchestrate Huerta's downfall. But many other factors, including

Huerta's growing unpopularity and the strength of the internal opposition to his brutal dictatorship, hastened his fall from power. After announcing his resignation on July 8, 1914, he quietly arranged his orderly and profitable departure to Spain.

CARRANZA AND THE CONSTITUTION OF 1917

Sadly, the insurgent leaders were unable to take advantage of Huerta's departure to negotiate among themselves there and then a peaceful settlement of their disputes, and to see Mexico embark on a new era of progress. Early steps in that direction—for example, a convention called in Aguascalientes, which was to have resulted in unanimous backing for Venustiano Carranza as president—collapsed in the face of the fierce rivalry between Carranza and Pancho Villa. In the end, a Villa candidate, Eulalio Gutiérrez, was named provisional president and, with support from Villa's army and Zapata, took office in Mexico City. Gutiérrez's tenure was short, however, as he was soon to be run out of Mexico City by the advancing army of Alvaro Obregón. Thwarted in his presidential ambitions, Carranza moved to Veracruz, where a sympathetic American government evacuated its military forces just in time to allow him to establish a provisional capital. Pancho Villa, declaring himself the true leader of the nation, established his headquarters in Chihuahua.

Meanwhile, President Wilson, understandably confused by this pantheon of revolutionary leaders, slowly came to the decision to continue to support the "Constitutionalist" government of Carranza, which he recognized as the true successor to Madero in October 1915. This move enraged the previously rather pro-American Pancho Villa, who had recently been severely trounced by Carranza in the Battle of Celaya. Villa first took his revenge on a party of U.S. mining company employees who were traveling by train from El Paso, Texas, to the Cusihuiriachic mine in Chihuahua. At the village of Santa Isabel, the railroad right-of-way was barricaded, and all fifteen Americans were removed from the train by Villa's troops and murdered in cold blood.

Villa followed this savage act by another: the invasion by some 500 *villistas* of the sleeping American town of Columbus, New Mexico, on the dawn of March 9, 1916. Before being driven off later in the day by a nearby U.S. Cavalry unit, they had murdered eighteen Americans, wounded many times that number, and burned several buildings in the town to the ground.[2]

There followed an unsuccessful effort by the U.S. Cavalry, led by Gen. John J. Pershing (shortly thereafter to command U.S. forces in Europe in World War I) to track down and capture Villa. But the wily rebel was at home in the difficult countryside and eluded capture. In the end Carranza, facing domestic criticism for allowing U.S. forces to operate in Mexico, asked that General Pershing's expeditionary force be withdrawn. This was done in January 1917, ending the last direct U.S. military intervention in the affairs of its southern neighbor. But Pershing's so-called "punitive expeditions" against Mexican villagers thought to be sheltering Villa added to the legacy of anti-Americanism in the Mexican psyche.

Carranza then turned his attention to the long-promised drafting of a new Mexican constitution. (The resulting Mexican Constitution of 1917 is still Mexico's governing document.) Though he took care in choosing the participants in a Constitutional Convention, it was soon clear that the delegates who met in Querétaro were more radical than Carranza would have wished; they incorporated into the document measures such as land reform, limits to the powers of the Church, and restrictions

---

[2] The author's grandfather, Dr. G.W.R. Smith, a physician and surgeon in nearby Mesilla Park, New Mexico, alerted by a railway telegrapher to the tragedy, drove immediately to the scene with several boxes of medical supplies and treated the wounded from both sides.

on the foreign ownership of property. But in the end, the constitution was adopted. Carranza was elected president and took office on May 1, 1917.

Carranza soon found himself embroiled in the international events of World War I. As the U.S. entered the war, he faced a great dilemma: Should Mexico join many other Latin American countries in breaking diplomatic relations with Germany and aligning itself with the U.S. and the Allies? Germany's foreign minister, Arthur Zimmerman, had another idea. In a famous telegram to Carranza in February 1917, he promised that, if Mexico were to side with the Central Powers, all of its territories lost in the Mexican War would be restored! Carranza wisely rejected the offer, although rather than join the Allies he declared Mexico's strict neutrality.[3]

Carranza then devoted himself to consolidating his position within Mexico. A campaign against the insurgent Zapata, resulting in thousands of casualties on both sides, was inconclusive. A frustrated Carranza successfully arranged for Zapata to be tricked into a meeting in April 1919 with a local military commander, and assassinated. But Carranza's success was to be short-lived: Only a few months later, he himself was shot to death, perhaps by one of his own guards, while on his way to exile after having lost a power struggle with Obregón. The motive for the slaying has never been fully established, though many felt that Obregón or one of his followers wanted to make sure that a potent opponent was permanently silenced.

The assassinations of Zapata and Carranza were but fleeting

---

[3] Another, earlier German plan, hatched in 1915, also failed. It called for smuggling the exiled Huerta back to Mexico to lead a counter-revolution—which, by engaging U.S. troops in the defense of Carranza's forces, would keep the Yanks from going to Europe should the U.S. enter the war. British intelligence uncovered the plot, enabling U.S. authorities to arrest Huerta on his way to Mexico through Texas. He remained in U.S. custody until his death from cirrhosis of the liver on January 13, 1916.

CLINT E. SMITH

Figure 2.2
A Mexican revolutionary stands firm against the encroaching
forces of imperialism. By José Clemente Orozco.

Figure 2.3
The victorious Pancho Villa, surrounded by his followers, poses uneasily
in the presidential chair with a wary Emiliano Zapata beside him.

scenes in the tragic decade from 1910 through 1920, when about a million citizens out of a population of 15 million lost their lives as a result of the violent conflict. The economic and social costs were terrible as well, ranging from the emigration of many professionals and skilled workers to the U.S. to neglected farms, destroyed industries and mines, and demolished public schools and hospitals.

ALVARO OBREGÓN AND THE BEGINNINGS OF PEACE

The election of Alvaro Obregón in Mexico City in 1920, combined with the deaths of Zapata and Carranza and the co-optation of Villa—who lived on a large *hacienda* in Canutillo, Chihuahua, until his assassination by a group of eight armed men in 1923—

ushered in a relatively peaceful era.[4] Mexico's economy began a slow recovery (it was not to revisit Porfirian levels until World War II) led by oil production, which reached 200 million barrels in 1922, making the country a world leader in oil and gas exports and providing a tax base for modest social progress.

While Obregón was slow in applying the more radical measures in the Constitution of 1917, such as agrarian reform or the national patrimony of oil and gas, he did make substantial headway in the fields of education and culture. He appointed a distinguished intellectual, José Vasconcelos, to the new cabinet position of secretary of public education. It was Vasconcelos who brought public education to Mexico's rural sectors. He recruited thousands of bright university students to leave the major cities and go off—often on muleback—to remote villages in the countryside, carrying with them boxes containing school supplies and perhaps fifty carefully selected books for teaching reading, writing, mathematics, and Mexican history.

Vasconcelos's philosophy was based not on the later, popular notion of preserving indigenous cultures but rather on the desirability of incorporating all the peoples of Mexico into one economic and political unit: the Mexican nation. This nation was to consist, in Vasconcelos's vision, of a cosmic race—*la raza cósmica*—that would prove a unique force in securing Mexico's future greatness. In any case, more than 1,000 schools were built during the first four years of Vasconcelos's term. Several thousand other communities were served by temporary schoolhouses located in modest village buildings.

Recognizing that the population was only 50 percent literate, Vasconcelos called on leading artists to tell Mexico's unique

---

[4] Historians are in disagreement about the motivation of the Villa assassination. Some believe it was a personal vendetta, but most seem to feel that it was politically motivated, perhaps in response to a threat by Villa to come out of exile and vie once again for national power.

story to its citizens. He commissioned three great muralists—Diego Rivera, husband of the artist Frida Kahlo; José Clemente Orozco, an introspective painter from Guadalajara; and the fiery Stalinist, David Alfaro Siqueiros—to cover the walls of government buildings all over Mexico with pictorial histories of famous events. These muralists (*los tres grandes*) and many others who are lesser known depicted the great civilizations of the Mayans and Aztecs, the coming of the Spaniards, the struggles for independence, and the Mexican Revolution in a way that made history memorable for the masses. Many of their great works—for example the murals of Rivera in the National Palace on Mexico City's main plaza (*el Zócalo*)—are still frequently visited by Mexicans and foreigners alike. In total, they represent one of the most important contributions to popular art of the 20th century.

RELATIONS WITH THE U.S. UNDER OBREGÓN

President Obregón soon found himself in the difficult position of dealing with one of America's most corrupt political regimes. Warren G. Harding's administration, dominated by the influence of such oil barons as Harry F. Sinclair and Edward L. Doheny, became enmeshed in the infamous Teapot Dome scandal. The oil and mining interests that had found scant support during the presidency of Woodrow Wilson were in their element with the pliable Harding and his corrupt secretary of the interior, Albert B. Fall. As a result of this influence, along with Obregón's refusal to abrogate the terms of the Mexican Constitution regarding oil ownership, the U.S. witheld its recognition of his government from 1920 until 1923. Finally, faced by growing internal security problems, Obregón initiated negotiations that at last appeased U.S. oil interests, and Mexico was granted formal diplomatic recognition.

That recognition—and Obregón's consequent ability to gain

credits for the import of needed military supplies and other material—came just in time, as a military revolt from the north, this time led by Adolfo de la Huerta of Sonora, had to be put down. This turned out to be the last serious effort at a violent change of government. Obregón was able, in 1924, to pass the presidential sash peacefully to his elected successor, Plutarco Elías Calles. Though much criticized by radical intellectuals, Obregón had performed successfully the delicate task of stabilizing his country and dealing with its difficult northern neighbor. A new era for Mexico had begun.

3 MEXICO GROWS AND DEVELOPS (1924–PRESENT)

The history of Mexico in the decade after the violent stage of the Revolution (Mexicans consider that the Revolution itself continues to this day) was written to a significant degree by President Plutarco Elías Calles, a liberal leader from Mexico's northern province of Sonora. Between 1924 and 1934, Calles built a solid political base for governance in Mexico, which is all the more remarkable when one considers the violent era which preceded it. Calles was able to enlist the support of agrarian reformers; the labor movement, headed by Luis Morones and his *Confederación Regional Obrera Mexicana* (CROM, or regional confederation of Mexican workers); and the business and industrial sectors.

However, Calles faced a difficult period of relations with

U.S. government officials during his early years. Neither the U.S. ambassador to Mexico, a businessman named James Sheffield, nor the secretary of state, Frank R. Kellogg, showed any understanding of Mexico or its problems. Sheffield believed that Anglo-Saxons had a duty to guide the natives of non-white countries (such as Mexico) to understand their interests and obligations. Kellogg was little better, announcing at one point that "Mexico is now on trial before the world. . . . We cannot countenance violation of her obligations and failure to protect U.S. citizens."

Calles, seeing the U.S. officials' approach as a threat to Mexico's sovereignty, reacted by strengthening Mexico's laws on national ownership of untapped oil and gas reserves (those being exploited at the time by foreign companies were on the basis of a fifty-year lease that, during the period of the leasehold, for all practical purposes amounted to outright ownership). He also succeeded in obtaining the departure of Sheffield with a minimum of fuss.

Fortunately, the new U.S. ambassador to Mexico was one of the best ever sent to that country. Dwight Morrow, though a senior partner at J. P. Morgan, soon proved his independence from the U.S. business and financial communities and his desire to improve U.S.-Mexico relations. The Morrows chose to live in a Mexican-style residence and traveled extensively through Mexico, learning its language and culture. In contrast to his predecessors, Morrow called publicly for dignity and mutual respect in the relationship between the two countries.[1]

Morrow early sought and achieved an easy, informal relationship with the sometimes prickly President Calles. The pair began a regular schedule of breakfasts together, capitalizing on

---

[1] Morrow's invitation of world-famous aviator Charles Lindbergh on a goodwill visit resulted, as it happened, in Lindbergh's marriage to the ambassador's daughter Anne.

Figure 3.1
President Calles with U.S. ambassador Morrow.

these occasions to resolve many issues without the encumbrances
of staffs and formal negotiations. Morrow also used his influence at the White House to tone down the Washington rhetoric
and to elicit key statements reaffirming U.S. recognition of
Mexico's sovereignty.

During this period, Calles's greatest difficulties were with the
right wing of the Church, and its *Cristeros*, armed bands of
campesinos centered in Jalisco and nearby areas in the west and
south of Mexico who attacked targets such as public schools
and murdered schoolteachers and other public employees with
the cry *¡Viva Cristo Rey!* (Long live Christ the King!).

The Constitution of 1917 had nationalized churches, forbidden foreign clergy, banned religious processions, and forbade priests and nuns from appearing in cassocks or habits. These rules were unevenly enforced, but Calles began to apply them with a vengeance. Calles saw the Church as the major enemy of reform, an obstacle to progress and modernization—and to the consolidation of his own power! In 1926 Calles required that all clergy be licensed. Local priests, particularly in western Mexico, incited peasants to begin a guerrilla war in the name of Christ. (Significantly, neither the *hacendados* nor the business community were much involved.) Violence erupted in several states.

Calles responded with further sanctions against the Church. He deported about two hundred foreign priests and nuns, closed all Church schools, and shut down more than seventy monasteries and convents. Government troops entered the scene and committed atrocities of their own against suspected *Cristeros*. Some governors organized paramilitary "red shirts" to attack priests and their supporters, and to burn churches. The Vatican disassociated the Church from the armed struggle and urged Catholics not to support the *Cristero* movement.

The result was a tragic standoff. Although the government had far greater force on its side, the conflict remained unresolved when Calles left the presidency in 1928. His elected successor, Obregón, was murdered by a *Cristero* fanatic, and the presidency went to one of Calles's proteges, Emilio Portes Gil. All this instability in Mexico was cause for concern on the part of Ambassador Morrow, who persuaded U.S. clerics with Vatican connections to act as informal mediators. Thus, Portes Gil and the Archbishop of Mexico were eventually able to come to an agreement—signed in the summer of 1929—effectively ending the *Cristero* insurgency, and churches were reopened, although isolated acts of fanaticism continued into the mid-1930s.

While a series of Calles loyalists (Portes Gil, Ortiz Rubio, and Gen. Abelardo Rodríguez) were serving as presidents, Calles was busily building the political institution that has governed Mexico for more than sixty years. In 1929, Calles organized the *Partido Nacional Revolucionario* (PNR) in a successful effort to reduce the power of local *caciques*, or political bosses, and to institutionalize the Revolution in a single, national party dedicated to its goals. The present name of the same party, the *Partido Revolucionario Institucional* (PRI), reflects this objective.

By 1930, the political stability that Mexico had long sought was at hand. The Church was under control; the military, labor, and business leaders had been co-opted into the PNR party mechanism; and the stage was set for the election of one of Mexico's most famous reformers, Lázaro Cárdenas, to the presidency.

CÁRDENAS, ROOSEVELT, AND THE OIL CRISIS

Cárdenas, who first achieved fame as a military leader during the Revolution, was actually a quiet man of deep personal commitment to social change. As governor of his native Michoacán (1928–32) he opened new schools and invited peasants and industrial workers to organize and work within the political system. He was able to improve conditions in Michoacán even as the worldwide Depression was hitting the Mexican economy.

This success called him to the attention of the PNR and its leader. Calles invited Cárdenas to run for the presidency, which he easily won in 1934. However, a disappointed Calles soon discovered that this new president was not another puppet. Far from it! When Calles began publicly to criticize the new regime, he suddenly found himself being flown off to the United States and permanent exile, never again to be a force on the Mexican political scene.

The balance of the Cárdenas term (1934–40) saw extensive educational reform and the building of thousands of schools throughout the country, the growth of the Mexican labor movement, and the breaking up of many giant *haciendas*, with the land given to *ejidos*, or peasant communities. But Cárdenas remains best known throughout the world for successfully taking on the United States and the powerful foreign oil companies that had exploited Mexican oilfields for decades without even minimal government control, which at least might have ensured that Mexicans received a fair share of the profits.

The election of Franklin D. Roosevelt to the U.S. presidency in 1933 began the era of the Good Neighbor policy toward Mexico and Latin America. During FDR's first year in office, U.S. military forces were withdrawn from Nicaragua and Haiti and a policy of non-intervention in Latin American countries was adopted. The new president's first ambassador to Mexico, Josephus Daniels, an old FDR friend and mentor, was a staunch supporter of the emerging inter-American system. Daniels established a personal friendship with Cárdenas, whose social programs Daniels enthusiastically likened to the New Deal. Though Daniels did voice concern about the need for prompt compensation for U.S. landowners suffering from Cárdenas's agrarian reform measures, relations in general between the two men, and the two countries, were excellent.

Thus it came as a shock when, on March 18, 1938, President Cárdenas signed an edict seizing the holdings of more than a dozen U.S. and all other foreign oil companies. Ambassador Daniels described the seizure as a "thunderbolt out of a blue sky." But Cárdenas believed there was ample justification for the action. The oil companies had for two years taken legal measures to stave off oil workers's demands for wage increases, and had refused to obey a Mexican Supreme Court edict upholding pay hikes that a government commission had recommended. Cárdenas, calling this intransigence a defiance of Mexico's national sovereignty, declared that his action was sanctioned by the Mexican Constitution.

International legal experts argued that Cárdenas's initial action on March 18 was tantamount to confiscation (under international law, wrongful seizure without immediate and adequate payment). At Daniels's urging he soon showed a willingness to negotiate the move as an expropriation, sanctioned by international law because it involves prompt and fair payment. These negotiations were onerous and protracted, but the process itself relieved some pressure.

Meanwhile, the newly created *Petróleos Mexicanos* (Pemex, the state oil agency), facing an Anglo-American boycott, began to sell oil to Germany, which was building up its reserves in anticipation of World War II. Ambassador Daniels and President Roosevelt were concerned about the intransigence of the oil companies, which they considered to be short-sighted in view of the crumbling world situation, and encouraged an early resolution of the issue. But it was not until November 19, 1941, virtually on the eve of America's entry into the war, that a final agreement was signed giving foreign companies a total of $105 million in compensation for their oil concessions—$81 million for British firms and $24 million for U.S. companies. The companies were undoubtedly somewhat unhappy at this conclusion; but at last, the efforts of Ambassador Daniels, who from the first had counseled both sides in the direction of moderation, and the world crisis combined to bring the matter to a close.

THE U.S. AND MEXICO IN WORLD WAR II

The atmosphere for a peaceful resolution of the oil company takeovers was improved by the Roosevelt administration's desire to get Mexico and Latin America on board as allies in what was clearly the coming war in Europe—a goal with which Cárdenas, an ardent anti-Fascist, was in sympathy. By the time Cárdenas left office in 1940, relations between the two countries were on a relatively even keel.

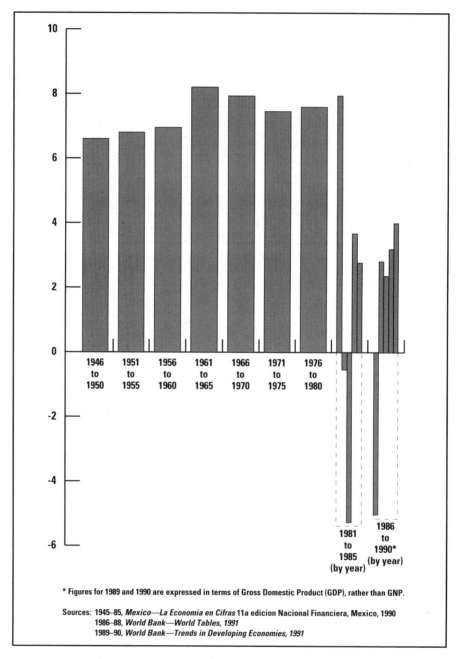

* Figures for 1989 and 1990 are expressed in terms of Gross Domestic Product (GDP), rather than GNP.

Sources: 1945–85, *Mexico—La Economia en Cifras* 11a edicion Nacional Financiera, Mexico, 1990
1986–88, *World Bank—World Tables, 1991*
1989–90, *World Bank—Trends in Developing Economies, 1991*

Figure 3.2
Real GNP Growth in Mexico, 1945–90

The charismatic Lázaro Cárdenas, still remembered by many as Mexico's greatest social reformer, was succeeded by the more conservative Gen. Manuel Avila Camacho. After hearing for years U.S. complaints about the "Reds" running Mexico, that country's citizens found it quite humorous that the U.S. representative attending Avila Camacho's inauguration, Vice President Henry Wallace, was in fact well to the left of Mexico's new president on the political spectrum!

This conservative reputation had actually helped Avila Camacho in his electoral campaign. Nominated by the government party at the behest of Cárdenas, Avila was opposed by the extremely conservative Juan Andreu Almazán of the *Partido de Acción Nacional* (PAN)—then, as now, Mexico's major conservative party, representing industrialists, landowners, the Church, and the growing upper-middle class, especially in northern Mexico. The PAN leadership had expected to run against Francisco Mugica, a fiery radical, and would probably have captured a broad range of moderate and conservative votes. But the contrast between Andreu Almazán and Avila Camacho was not dramatic enough to have much popular impact, and the better-organized PNR won an easy victory.

During his term in office (1940–46), Avila Camacho was preoccupied by World War II and its impact on his foreign and domestic policies. His policy of friendship with the U.S. and the Allies at first gained him the enmity of the Mexican left—at least until the summer of 1941, when Hitler's attack on the Soviet Union changed some leftists' minds. On December 8, 1941, the day after Pearl Harbor, Avila Camacho broke relations with Germany, Japan, and Italy; on May 24, 1942, after two Mexican oil tankers had been torpedoed by U-Boats, he declared war on the Axis powers. Mexico's contributions to the war effort included sending a courageous fighter squadron to the Far East under General MacArthur's command; the export of vast quantities of strategic metals and minerals to the U.S.;

and the dispatching of some 200,000 Mexican *braceros* (laborers) to the U.S. to replace American farm and industrial workers who had joined the military services.

By 1946 the PNR, having changed its name to the *Partido Revolucionario Institucional* (PRI), was ready to embark on a new era (roughly 1946–82) in which it would base its popularity and strength on Mexico's continuing and unbroken economic growth and development. World War II had encouraged a rapid industrial expansion led by young, often U.S.-trained engineers and entrepreneurs. These activities were centered in Monterrey, Guadalajara, and Mexico City. The state development bank, Nacional Financiera, created in the Cárdenas era, was expanded by the addition of a large, well-trained technical staff; the country's financial and planning infrastructure were thereby markedly improved. Mexico's economic renaissance led to three decades of almost unbroken real economic growth, averaging more than 5 percent a year, with real GNP doubling during the years 1946–58.

THE POSTWAR YEARS

Mexican historians have made an important point about U.S. foreign policy in the years following World War II, from which the U.S. emerged as the most powerful nation in the world. This analysis revolves around the fact that the U.S. chose to perceive relations with Latin America, including Mexico, in an international security context, while turning its attention in the international economic arena to war-shattered Europe. There was no counterpart to the Marshall Plan in the developing countries of the Western Hemisphere.

But even without the economic assistance that would have been provided by a Latin American Marshall Plan, the Mexican economy continued to grow robustly under the leadership of a new, private-sector-oriented president, Miguel Alemán Valdés

(1946–52). Alemán, the first civilian in decades to be elected president of Mexico, also received the first visit by a U.S. president to Mexico City when Harry Truman arrived in March 1947.

Recognizing that rapid industrialization could not take place without an adequate infrastructure in place, Alemán embarked

Figure 3.3
Library, National University of Mexico. Mosaic mural by Juan O'Gorman.

early in his administration on a series of massive public-works projects including dams, power stations, electrification, telecommunications networks, and highways. Pemex doubled its production during the Alemán years and provided subsidized oil and gas to industrial users. The huge new campus of the *Universidad Nacional Autónoma de México* (UNAM, the national university) was built at the edge of rapidly growing Mexico City.

Despite the economic growth and development that marked Alemán's administration, his successor, Adolfo Ruiz Cortines, came to office facing a number of serious challenges. Ruiz Cortines focused the first months of his presidency on pressing social issues such as the full enfranchisement of women into the political and electoral process, a goal that was accomplished during his administration. During his term in office (1952–58), he also vastly expanded the Mexican version of Social Security. But despite his careful administration, social problems grew in intensity, exacerbated by Mexico's rapid population increases and stagnant real wages for workers, whose salary increases were obliterated by the inflation that was creeping into the economy; for during Ruiz Cortines's last years in office, massive public spending projects were paid for by an overactive printing press. The crowning blow to his administration was a protracted series of strikes by railroad and other transportation workers, all put down with considerable police and paramilitary violence.

Ruiz Cortines's relations with the U.S., in general friendly and uneventful, were dramatically marred in June 1954 by the U.S. intervention in Guatemala to overthrow the reformist president Jacobo Arbenz. A leftist democrat determined to pursue a land reform program that threatened the considerable holdings of the wealthy *hacendados* (and of the United Fruit Company), Arbenz was overthrown in a CIA-supported coup by Col. Carlos Castillo Armas. The CIA's support was widely denounced by Mexicans, thousands of whom demonstrated against it on the streets, as being all too typical of past *yanqui* interventions.

LÓPEZ MATEOS, CUBA, AND CHAMIZAL

In 1958, Mexicans elected one of their youngest and most charismatic presidents, Adolfo López Mateos, to succeed Ruiz Cortines. Sometimes compared to John F. Kennedy, who was elected to the U.S. presidency in 1960, López Mateos was 47 years old, energetic, and very popular, his service as secretary of labor having gained him the reputation of concern for the welfare of workers and farmers.

López Mateos (1958–64) found his principal challenges to be in the arena of foreign policy. One of the first of these was the Cuban Revolution of 1959, which saw Fidel Castro coming to power after overthrowing the right-wing dictatorship of Fulgencio Batista. Castro was seen initially throughout the Western Hemisphere, including the United States, as a heroic figure who had brought freedom to a people long suffering under the yoke of a tyrant. But it soon became obvious that Castro, with the strong support of the Soviet Union, was in fact intent on establishing in Latin America a Communist dictatorship of the Eastern European variety.

Soon most of the hemisphere's constituent countries were taking firm, multilateral measures—breaking relations and imposing economic sanctions, for example—to curb the Castro regime's efforts to consolidate its own hold on Cuba and export arms and the Communist revolution to other countries in the area. But despite the urging of the United States and other Latin American neighbors, Mexico, bound by its historic policy of nonintervention and its own revolutionary tradition, found itself unable to vote for several Organization of American States measures condemning Cuba and expelling it from this regional body. Within a short time, Mexico found itself the only Latin American country maintaining diplomatic relations or even regular air links with Cuba.

Surprisingly, the Mexican approach to the Cuban situation

did not prove to be a serious handicap to the U.S.-Mexico relationship. In fact, the period of the López Mateos regime, during which several Cuban crises (such as the abortive Bay of Pigs invasion and the missile crisis of October 1963) unfolded, was a very successful one vis-à-vis the United States. Certainly, the most dramatic and enduring success was the joint resolution of a boundary dispute that had festered for more than a century.

In 1864, due to a shift in the course of the Rio Grande (*Rio Bravo*) near the border towns of El Paso, Texas, and Ciudad Juárez, Mexico, some six hundred acres of what had been Mexican territory (known as Chamizal) became part of the United States. Numerous commissions, convened from time to time over the ensuing hundred years, had been unable to reach agreement on a new boundary. But talks undertaken between López Mateos and Kennedy in 1962, when the U.S. president made a state visit to Mexico City, led to an agreement between Mexico's Secretariat of Foreign Relations and the U.S. State Department. The agreement—which called for a permanent channeling of the river through the disputed area, the construction of an international park, and a new international bridge connecting El Paso and Ciudad Juárez—was approved by both countries' legislatures. (In November 1963 President Kennedy was assassinated; the final pact was actually signed by Kennedy's successor, Lyndon B. Johnson, and López Mateos in September 1964.)

On the domestic scene, too, López Mateos moved adroitly. Responding to critics' charges of PRI dominance in the legislative branch, he had Mexico's electoral procedures modified to permit the participation of such opposition parties as the conservative PAN and the socialist *Partido Popular Socialista* (PPS). While these and other moves in the direction of electoral reform did demonstrate some sensitivity on López Mateos's part to the need for reform, they did little to diminish the power of the PRI at the presidential level.

Figure 3.4
Presidents Johnson and López Mateos at the Chamizal Ceremony in 1964.

PRESIDENT DÍAZ ORDAZ AND THE TLATELOLCO MASSACRE

López Mateos led Mexico skillfully for six years, handling the Cuban crises well and developing good relations with a series of U.S. presidents—Eisenhower, Kennedy, and Johnson. He left the presidential office in the hands of his secretary of the interior, Gustavo Díaz Ordaz, a dour, unimaginative conservative who soon found himself in a tense political situation beyond his capacity to manage. The results were tragic. Perhaps especially because Díaz Ordaz's tenure (1964–70) was in most ways undistinguished, he will certainly be best remembered for his responsibility for the horror of Tlatelolco.

Mexico was proud to be chosen as the host for the 1968 Olympic Games, and Díaz Ordaz was determined that nothing should interfere with their complete success. Yet on the eve of the games, numerous large groups of Mexican high-school and university students attempted anti-government demonstrations around Mexico City. Díaz Ordaz ordered immediate and severe police and military actions against the students; thousands were arrested and beaten. The government's action, of course, served only to heat up the situation. Within days, tens of thousands of high school and university students, professors, and even parents were demonstrating against the Díaz Ordaz regime.

In response, Díaz Ordaz ordered the Mexican army to occupy the university and sent thousands of members of his security forces to cover possible sites for further demonstrations. Inevitably, tragedy struck. On the night of October 2, 1968, security forces stationed at *la Plaza de las Tres Culturas* in Tlatelolco (an old area of downtown Mexico City where the Secretariat of Foreign Relations is located) opened fire on students and their supporters with automatic weapons. To this date, there is considerable debate on how many were massacred that night, though responsible estimates are in the range of two to four hundred, with more than two thousand arrested. Whatever the real figure, the trauma of Tlatelolco on the Mexican people is still not fully behind them, just as Americans have not entirely forgotten the similar tragedy of Kent State, which, though with far fewer casualties as a result of young National Guardsmen firing on students, was symbolic of the era.

THE ECHEVERRÍA YEARS

Luis Echeverría Alvarez, who as secretary of the interior in the Díaz Ordaz administration also bore considerable responsibility for the Tlatelolco tragedy, was nominated by the PRI in 1970 to succeed Díaz Ordaz. Faced with the huge task of regaining credibility for the party—and the government—after Tlatelolco, Echeverría, though running against very weak opposition from the left and right, traversed the country, visiting more than eight hundred cities and towns and touring thousands of rural areas during the campaign. While up to that point Echeverría had been considered quite conservative, the rhetoric of his speeches now began to take on a nationalistic, leftist hue—what he called "revolutionary nationalism." Rural development became a major theme; innumerable promises were made along the campaign trail to bring roads, electricity, water, and schools to impoverished parts of the country.

To his great credit, Echeverría made a startling turnaround in the vitally important field of family planning. Long an opponent of birth control, he now gave it his endorsement, undertaking a joint public- and private-sector campaign that has continued through successive administrations. As a result, the annual rate of population growth in Mexico has dropped from 3.3 percent in 1970 to 2.0 percent in 1990. Without Echeverría's initiative, there is no doubt that Mexico's population explosion, serious enough as it is, would now be considerably worse.

Despite Echeverría's calls for domestic social reforms, the aftermath of Tlatelolco continued to be felt. Terrorist groups perpetrated a number of kidnappings, including those of U.S. consul general Terrance Leonhardy in Guadalajara and the PRI senator from Guerrero, Ruben Figueroa. Eugenio Garza Sada, Mexico's leading industrialist, was shot to death in a botched kidnapping attempt in Monterrey. A terrorist group organized by former university student leaders and led by Lucio Cabañas was responsible for several bank robberies and kidnappings. In the end, it took Echeverría more than a year and the assignment of more than 10,000 army troops to neutralize Cabañas's group. Cabañas himself was killed in a clash with army special forces.

In spite of—or more likely, because of—the troubles and mistrust that plagued his administration on the domestic front, Echeverría made an extraordinary effort to propel himself and Mexico onto the world scene. Speaking as much for internal effect as internationally, Echeverría told a startled nation and world that Mexico was "following a path between capitalism and socialism." His bid for leadership in the Third World involved him in whirlwind travels to Africa, the Far East, and elsewhere. He promoted a "Charter of Economic Rights and Duties of States" which was passed by the U.N. General Assembly, but had little practical effect, since, as one critic noted, it gave the developing countries all the rights and the developed countries all the duties, without suggesting any means of collaboration for mutual benefit.

In the end, Echeverría's international campaign, including an unsuccessful bid to be elected secretary general of the United Nations, was to have little global impact, much less restore confidence in him as a national leader. One of his actions was particularly disastrous. Perhaps in a desire to win Arab friendship, he lent Mexico's voice to a 1975 U.N. General Assembly resolution equating Zionism with racism. This caper had a devastating effect. Hundreds of U.S. and European tourist organizations organized a 1976 boycott of Mexican resorts, seriously affecting Mexico's two-billion-dollar tourist industry, on which many thousands of jobs depend. Dozens of Mexican resort hotels stood near-empty at the height of the season, resulting in considerable economic losses.

During his last years in office, Echeverría resorted to public-spending policies, including public works, social welfare, and subsidies, that soon plagued the country with growing inflation—more than 20 percent a year at one point—and a trade deficit in 1975 of $3.5 billion. A 1973 law restricting foreign private investment had a chilling effect on the business climate both at home and abroad. His final acts in office—for example, an *ex post facto* approval of illegal land seizures by peasants in Sonora; orchestrating the removal of a principal press critic, Julio Scherer, editor of the respected Mexico City daily newspaper *Excelsior*; and a too-long-deferred devaluation of the peso—

did nothing to redeem his administration.

The troubled regime, which had begun in the shadow of the Tlatelolco massacre and never did regain the trust of students and intellectuals, ended with a crisis of confidence on the part of the middle-class business and professional communities; in his last weeks, Echeverría faced the flight of several billions of dollars by Mexican businessmen and investors sick of being excoriated by Echeverría as betrayers of the national patrimony. Nor had the president in any way improved U.S.-Mexico relations or portrayed Mexico in a serious light on the world stage.

JOSÉ LÓPEZ PORTILLO: OIL, DEBT, AND CORRUPTION

José López Portillo, an aristocratic intellectual who served as finance minister in the latter part of the Echeverría administration, took office on December 1, 1976. Though he inherited a mismanaged economy (for which he bore some responsibility as well), he soon found himself in what appeared to be a most fortunate position. At a time when the Arab oil producers and the Organization of Petroleum Exporting Countries were driving up the price of oil to historic highs, and Americans were waiting in long lines at gas stations, Mexico found itself sitting on proven reserves of oil estimated at more than 60 billion barrels. This compared with only 42 billion barrels in the United States and 228 billion in incredibly oil-rich Saudi Arabia.

Mexico's economic problems seemed to be resolved forever. The country, López Portillo believed, had only to pump out the requisite amount of oil and sell it abroad to bring wealth into his treasury. Oil production rose from 800,000 barrels a day in 1976 to 2.3 million barrels a day in 1980. Mexico's trade surpluses in this era of rapidly rising oil prices were the envy of the non-oil-exporting world. "The world is now divided into two camps: nations that produce oil, and nations that do not. Mexico is a nation that does!" declared López Portillo.

Conventional wisdom had it that the price of a barrel of oil would soon hit $50. In the brief but heady days of Mexico's oil supremacy, López Portillo greatly enjoyed flaunting his perceived new power on the international stage, ignoring the boycott of the Moscow Olympic games in 1980 after the USSR's invasion of Afghanistan, and taking the opportunity presented by President Carter's state visit to Mexico to needle the visiting U.S. leader about America's "past deceits" and warn him against such actions in the future. López Portillo also officially recognized the legitimacy of the insurgents in El Salvador and made state visits to Cuba, the Soviet Union, Bulgaria, and the People's Republic of China.

Even early on in the López Portillo administration (1976–82), however, knowledgeable observers found the economic situation disturbing. Though oil exports were up dramatically, so was unemployment. Mexico's resources were flowing to capital-intensive petroleum exploitation, while slower growth in more-labor-intensive manufacturing and other sectors failed to provide enough jobs for the 800,000 young Mexicans entering the job force each year.

López Portillo's response was to embark on myriad government spending programs of unparalled magnitude, driving Mexico—able to borrow because of the oil boom and its petroleum and gas reserves—deeply into foreign debt. This borrowing and spending spree gave a brief illusion of economic dynamism, with real GNP growth of more than 8 percent in 1981 and 1982 (see Fig. 3.2); but, coinciding with the world oil bust of the early 1980s, the binge left Mexico desperate and virtually bankrupt. In August 1982, Mexican negotiators had to fly to Washington to arrange an international bailout.

On the morning of August 12, 1982, newly appointed finance minister Jesús Silva Herzog, who was much respected in world financial institutions, called U.S. treasury secretary Donald Regan, Federal Reserve Board chairman Paul Volcker, and

Jacques de Larosiere, managing director of the International Monetary Fund, with a compelling message: Mexico had run out of reserves and could not meet its international financial obligations, including interest payments on its $80 billion foreign debt, after Friday, August 13. He received an urgent invitation to Washington.

Though perhaps tempted by López Portillo's earlier arrogance to let him stew in the economic disaster he had created, U.S. and world financial leaders in fact acted quickly to contain the damage. Mexico's crisis was unprecedented in size and, if not resolved, could have the severest impact on the world's financial markets. It was only after an extraordinary effort over several weeks that the U.S. government, led by ambassador to Mexico John Gavin (a personal friend of President Reagan), Regan, and Volcker, along with private bank lenders represented by William Rhodes, a senior officer at Citibank, were able to negotiate a set of measures with the Mexicans: advance purchase of Mexican oil for the U.S. Strategic Oil Reserves; Treasury and Federal Reserve lines of support; a stretching out of payments on the commercial bank debt; the negotiation of an IMF standby agreement (which López Portillo at first opposed because under its terms funds would be made available only if Mexico undertook needed internal economic restructuring); and import credits for grains and basic foodstuffs. The package met Mexico's $20 billion need, and the crisis was, for the time being at least, averted.

The decline in the Mexican economy was exacerbated by the widespread corruption of the López Portillo administration. Indeed, Mexicans were distressed, if not exactly shocked, to hear that in his last year in office, the president had constructed four large mansions for himself and his family in an elegant part of Mexico City. Though this was the tip of the iceberg of corruption during his administration, it was symbolic of it.

But even more seriously, the López Portillo regime's borrow-

and-spend binge left Mexico facing its worst economic crisis in modern history. During his last year in office, profligate debt-financed government spending so darkened the business climate that Mexican and foreign businessmen fell all over themselves in shipping many billions of dollars out of the country. López Portillo responded by attempting a series of financial controls that resulted in a huge devaluation of the peso (from 26 to 100 to the dollar in a year's time). But he saved the greatest disaster for the end of his regime. In September 1982 López Portillo, in a tearful address to the country, nationalized the banking system, fired the respected head of Mexico's central bank, and embarked on a series of draconian exchange-control regulations that were, given the porous nature of the U.S.-Mexico border, utterly ineffective.

DE LA MADRID: A PERIOD OF PATIENT REBUILDING

Miguel de la Madrid Hurtado, while not a seasoned politician, was an economist and public-policy specialist with degrees from the National University of Mexico and Harvard, and was un-usually well qualified to take over the governance of Mexico late in 1982. Casting aside advice to repudiate Mexico's foreign debt, which had grown to a staggering $90 billion during López Portillo's administration, de la Madrid elected instead to nego-tiate the foreign-debt payment. He also embarked on a domes-tic-austerity program designed to bring Mexico slowly back to stability and, in the end, to a resumption of real economic growth.

The new Mexican president instituted drastic reductions in the public-sector budget, cutting 50,000 government jobs in the first year of his administration, reducing federal subsidies on most foodstuffs, and selling off a number of money-losing state enterprises. Abandoning the attempts of López Portillo to intro-duce exchange controls, he adopted a policy that, by means of small daily corrections, kept the peso at a reasonable rate of exchange with the dollar. He assembled a world-class economic team, headed by finance minister Silva Herzog and *Banco de México* (the central bank) director Miguel Mancera, to ensure the success of his international-finance efforts.

In a dramatic opening of the Mexican economy, the de la Madrid administration eschewed the protectionist, closed policies of the past and brought Mexico into the General Agreement on Tariffs and Trade (the GATT), an international body dedicated to lowering trade barriers. Mexico adopted a much more open policy regarding foreign ownership of Mexican enterprises and began to encourage, on a case-by-case basis, foreign investments that would bring needed new technology and jobs to Mexico.

Perhaps recognizing that economic reform alone could not rebuild public confidence shattered over the previous two administrations, de la Madrid moved to confront the corruption of the past. This led to the arrest and conviction of several leading figures of previous administrations, including the former director of Pemex, the state oil agency. Though for reasons of tradition, and perhaps political reality, de la Madrid did not seek to indict a previous president, he was able to make a convincing case for the need to reduce the rampant corruption of the recent past.

President de la Madrid was also faced with a crisis of the old political order. Before 1982, the apparently robust Mexican economy, with its sustained annual growth rates of 6 percent or better per year and an expanding middle class to which many could aspire, had muted all criticism of the autocratic nature of the PRI leadership. The economic crisis changed this dramatically, and de la Madrid was faced with the challenge of instituting political reforms at a time when doing so was made more difficult by a bad economic situation. Such reforms, long urged by the leadership of the conservative PAN as well as by the splinter parties of the left (not yet united in the dramatic way they would be in 1988), were clearly overdue.

De la Madrid's first effort in the direction of political reform came early in his administration and proceeded along three fronts: a call for free and fair elections across the nation and at all levels, a restraining arm de la Madrid himself placed on local political *caciques* traditionally loyal to the PRI, and improved access of opposition candidates to the media. These moves resulted in a number of victories for the PAN's mayoral candidates in Mexico's northern cities. The strong showing by the PAN stimulated the PRI apparatus to select better-qualified candidates capable of winning a free election. De la Madrid also instituted important election reforms that served to increase the number of opposition party representatives in the Mexican Congress.

On balance, and despite a disastrous earthquake in the autumn of 1985 that rocked Mexico City in the midst of his presidential term (1982–88), de la Madrid did manage to bring stability to the Mexican economy and to set the stage for the real growth that was to come under his chosen successor, Carlos Salinas de Gortari. A close political collaborator and cabinet secretary, Salinas was dedicated to building on de la Madrid's progress in opening the Mexican economy, restoring economic growth, and permitting greater pluralism in the Mexican political system.

But no sooner had Salinas won the PRI nomination than a powerful element within the PRI central apparatus, opposed to the continuation of de la Madrid's international economic policies, elected to leave the party. One of this group's leaders was Cuauhtémoc Cárdenas, the charismatic son of former president Lázaro Cárdenas. The young Cárdenas and his fellow-members of what they called the *corriente democrática* ("democratic current") formed a mainly leftist coalition party, the *Partido Revolucionario Democrático* (PRD), and in the presidential election of 1988 Cárdenas ran in a three-way race against Salinas and a strong and popular figure from PAN, Manuel Clouthier. The results surprised many seasoned observers of the Mexican political scene. After some whirring and clicking, the official government computers gave Salinas 50 percent of the vote, with 33 percent going to Cárdenas and 16 percent to Clouthier. Although one might question whether Salinas actually obtained a majority of the vote, most objective analysts believe that he obtained a clear plurality and was thus the legitimate victor in the election. (This is, however, still hotly disputed by the opposition.)

Another notable aspect of the 1988 elections was the victory by the PRD in two senatorial elections, both of them in the Federal District, the Mexican equivalent of the District of Columbia. The seats went to two members of Cárdenas's *corriente democrática*. In total, 240 of the 500 seats in Mexico's Chamber of Deputies went to opposition parties (mostly to the PRD and the PAN), leaving the PRI with 260 seats—its slimmest majority of all time.

And that was not all. In July 1989 the governorship of Baja California Norte went to the PAN candidate, Ernesto Ruffo Appel. This was the first time the PRI had lost a gubernatorial election since its founding in the wake of the Revolution. On November 1, 1989, after giving his *Informe* (State of the Union message) in Mexico City, President Salinas flew to Baja California to attend Governor Ruffo's inauguration—an unprecedented occurrence in Mexican political history. (Annoyed by this display of political warmth between the PRI and the PAN, the *cardenistas* quickly claimed that in contrast, the PRI had stolen the gubernatorial election from the PRD candidate in Cárdenas's home state of Michoacán.)

SALINAS DE GORTARI: MEXICO PREPARES FOR THE 21ST CENTURY

It is far too simple to label Cuauhtémoc Cárdenas as a leftist reformer and Salinas as the inheritor of the tradition of the

Revolutionary Family that founded the PRI. In fact, as we have seen, it was Cárdenas's father, Lázaro, who was one of the most important members of the Revolutionary Family. It can be argued that the Cárdenas candidacy in 1988 more nearly represented a continuation of traditional Mexican politics, with its base in economic nationalism, state controls, and a suspicion of the outside world in general and its often irksome northern neighbor in particular. Certainly an important underlying theme of the Cárdenas campaign was that the PRI—the party of the Revolution—had been captured from the top by a group of highly educated *técnicos* enamored of free-market economics, and was being led off in a dangerous direction. By inference, a vote for Cárdenas was a vote for the traditions his revered father espoused. This campaign strategy gained him considerable support in the countryside, often controlled by an older generation of rural politicians loyal to Lázaro Cárdenas and the old order, and among members of the industrial unions, notably the petroleum workers, whose special privileges inherited from the Lázaro Cárdenas era were seen to be at risk. Under this scenario, it was the Salinas group within the PRI that represented the changing direction of the parties and the modernization of Mexican economic and political structures along the path first taken by de la Madrid in the mid-1980s.

When President Salinas took his oath of office, two major clouds were still hanging over the recent Mexican past: the Tlatelolco tragedy in 1968, with its political fallout; and the debt crisis of 1982, with its legacy of austerity and decline in living standards. The former epitomized the end of an era of political stability that had extended over four decades; the latter revealed the bankruptcy of the economic policies of the 1970s that had paid for economic growth with a deficit-spending spree that brought Mexico to its knees on the international financial stage. The new president was fortunate in being insulated to some degree from these epochal events—by the passage of time in one case, and by the shrewd austerity program of his predecessor, Miguel de la Madrid, in the other.

Salinas's anti-corruption campaign was not long in coming to the fore. Many Mexican citizens were startled when, early in his administration, government forces arrested Joaquín Hernández Galicia, the notorious and powerful head of the huge *Petróleos Mexicanos* labor union. This was followed in short order by the arrest, on financial fraud charges, of the former head of the Mexico City Stock Exchange, and by other arrests, prosecutions, and convictions of lesser fry.

Since taking office, Salinas has wasted no time in expanding the economic programs that marked de la Madrid's term in office. His steps to continue the modernization of the Mexican economy have included rapid privatization of the state telephone monopoly, major steel mills and mining complexes, and the national airline. In a reversal of López Portillo's nationalization of the banking industry, an orderly return of banks and other financial institutions to private control was initiated early in Salinas's term. This measure alone resulted in an estimated $10 billion in capital returning to Mexico during 1990–91—a sure sign of a revival in investor confidence since the dark days of the López Portillo regime, when at least three times that amount fled abroad. As we shall see in Chapter 7, Salinas also has liberalized import restrictions and encouraged the flow of investment from the U.S. and abroad. He has instituted tax reforms and cut the public-sector deficit dramatically. And certainly one of his most important actions has been a successful renegotiation of Mexico's foreign debt, whereby more than five hundred creditors consented to a series of measures that effectively reduced Mexico's obligations by more than 10 percent.

Much structural change in the Mexican economy was still required, however, perhaps most significantly in the agricultural sector. In 1990, the net agricultural deficit on Mexico's balance of trade was about $4 billion. The *ejido* system of the

Mexican Revolution remained largely untouched and stood as a bar to internationally competitive agro-industry. This *minifundia*, or small communal landholding system, had not permitted the development of a modern agricultural economy.

On November 1, 1991, President Salinas addressed these issues in his State of the Union message. Some joint ventures between *ejidos* and Mexican investors have been allowed in agricultural zones—particularly in northern Mexico, where the atmosphere is more conducive to such arrangements, but also in the more sensitive (and impoverished) southern state of Chiapas. Until economic modernization reaches the Mexican farm on a far more massive scale, however, the country will have to continue to import food.

While his transformation of the agricultural sector (described in detail in Chapter 7) is a striking example of domestic reform, Salinas has moved in other important areas as well. Moving beyond the anticlerical shadow of the 1917 Revolution, he has granted legal recognition to the Roman Catholic Church, legitimized parochial-school education, allowed priests to vote, and permitted the Church to own property. The move also allows religious organizations of all denominations access to newpapers, radio, and television for the first time in more than seventy years. The most immediate effect will be on primary and secondary education, where a large number of Church-financed parochial schools are expected to be operating again in the near future, easing some of the pressure on overcrowded public schools and providing students with improved facilities.

This move parallels a strong effort to introduce structural reform to the Mexican public-education system, evidenced by President Salinas's January 1992 appointment of a trusted member of his team, Ernesto Zedillo Ponce de León, as secretary of public education. Zedillo had previously served as secretary of programs and budget (roughly equivalent to the head of the Office of Management and Budget in the U.S. government), but

A GIANT STEP FORWARD IN SOCIAL REFORM

A counterpoint to President Salinas's anti-corruption program is a social and economic development program with an annual budget that has grown from $2 billion in 1990 to an estimated $6 billion in 1992: the *Programa Nacional de Solidaridad*, or PRONASOL. Directed at the poorest economic areas, both rural and urban, PRONASOL actively encourages the emergence of community leaders who can decide for themselves what a town, village, or barrio's greatest needs are, and then receive, through PRONASOL's representatives, the government support needed to accomplish these goals—whether they be potable water, schools and playgrounds, roads, medical centers, or even sports facilities.

There is no doubt that this program is having a dramatic effect on thousands of communities in every state of Mexico. Some observers believe it explains the PRI victories in the August 1991 local elections. By the end of 1991, PRONASOL had provided decent water to 20 million Mexicans; hundreds of thousands of village streets were paved; more than one million children were enrolled in newly built schools; and a half-million small farmers and entrepreneurs had benefited from the *Fondo de Solidaridad para la Producción*, the Solidarity Production Fund, which helped them finance, grow, and market crops (e.g., coffee) and renewable resources (e.g., quality woods from the rainforest).

The underlying principle of PRONASOL is *Ayúdate, que yo te ayudaré* —or, roughly translated, PRONASOL will help those who help themselves. From a political point of view, of course, there is much advantage to be gained by the recruitment of authentic community leaders into projects that associate them with the government representatives of PRONASOL. But even with such successes, Salinas and his supporters of reform within the PRI still face considerable obstructionism from entrenched elements within the party structure. To battle this current, the president recently appointed a senator and close associate, Donaldo Colosio, to be the first minister of social development, with special responsibility for PRONASOL and a bundle of related social programs.

With its focus on the needs of the weakest members of society, PRONOSAL is President Salinas's major effort under the domestic rubric he calls *liberalismo social*, or social liberalism. This effort echoes the recommendations contained in his Harvard University doctoral thesis, based on field research in several of Mexico's less developed states.

much of the importance of his position was diminished by Salinas's decision—also announced in January—to transfer that department to the Treasury, headed by Pedro Aspe. This move made Aspe, a leading architect of Salinas's economic reforms, the second-most-powerful figure in Mexico.

President Salinas has also moved forward, although not as fast as many critics would wish, in the area of political liberalization. In July 1989 the PRI, the PAN, and some smaller parties in the Mexican Congress (the PRD was notable by its absence) jointly created a federal code of electoral procedures and set up a non-governmental electoral commission. Subsequently, measures to improve electoral fairness—such as a modernized process of voter registration and identification, poll-watching, and vote counting—have been instituted. While these steps in themselves have not wiped out voter fraud, they have certainly made it more difficult.

In an extraordinary session in September 1990, party members approved a dramatic series of changes within the PRI itself: secret ballots for internal elections; making PRI membership voluntary rather than compulsory for members of party-affiliated unions and rural workers organizations; and increased grass-roots influence in naming party candidates, which, it is hoped, will produce more attractive representatives. These moves were a clear victory for Salinas and others interested in modernizing the PRI, but they left many old-timers disgruntled; a few of these shortly resigned and joined the PRD.

Nowhere has President Salinas's political courage and conviction been demonstrated more than in his determination, from the beginning of his administration, to improve Mexico's relations with the United States. As president-elect, he met in Houston, Texas, with fellow president-elect George Bush and senior aides from both sides. The two men hit it off almost immediately, and their mutual confidence has had a dramatic and favorable effect on relations between the two countries.

By far the most dramatic move in recent United States-Mexico relations occurred on June 11, 1990, when Bush and Salinas jointly announced a schedule for the successful completion of a U.S.-Mexico Free Trade Agreement. After six months of intensive activity on the part of both U.S. and Mexican trade negotiators, the two presidents met again in November 1990 to confirm their commitment to achieving an agreement as quickly as possible. During the November summit it was also announced that Mexico was being granted a $1 billion credit with the Export-Import Bank of the United States (Ex-Im Bank) for petroleum exploration and exploitation. As the Ex-Im Bank traditionally makes loans only to U.S. suppliers and sub-contractors, this news was heartening; it was further evidence that the nationalization of the oil industry in 1938, which relegated U.S. firms to marginal participation in the Mexican petroleum industry, is now consigned to the past.

For the U.S., this development has positive national-security implications. Expansion activity by Pemex, with consequent greater production capacity, relieves the tensions caused by regional crises such as in the Persian Gulf, where U.S. oil imports are threatened. This is true for two reasons: It permits the Mexicans, if they wish, to increase actual production for sales on the U.S. market or to the U.S. Strategic Petroleum Reserve; and, by increasing potential production capacity (called surge capacity), it puts Mexico in a position to react in an international oil emergency by immediately increasing production to meet Western Hemisphere needs.

The decision on Mexico's part to seek financing from Ex-Im Bank for the oil industry was controversial in Mexico. Critics feared it was the first step toward *yanquis* getting back into a business Lázaro Cárdenas had driven them out of. But others saw it as a way not only of increasing Mexico's export potential, but also of ensuring that Mexico would have the oil and gas to meet the growing needs of its own improving economy.

THE AUGUST 1991 ELECTIONS AND BEYOND

The broadest criticism President Salinas has received during the course of his administration has concerned the pace of political reform. The president has invited some of this by giving first priority to needed economic reforms, with political changes, however necessary in the long term, coming second. One critic, Nobel laureate Octavio Paz, warned the young president that if reforms did not come soon, the PRI would remain an obstacle to democratization and modernization of the Mexican society.

The August 1991 elections provided evidence that change is possible. The PRI, which had greatly improved its local campaign organizations and won back a more robust majority in the Congress, ceded (after protests, to be sure) the governorships of three contested states—Guanajuato, San Luis Potosí, and Tabasco. Observers saw the direct presidential hand in these decisions, which addressed domestic and international sensitivity to the issue of political openness. Local election results in late 1991 and early 1992 have also reflected a growing pluralism, with gains by the PRD in such states as Michoacán and by the PAN mainly in the north. In short, Mexico remains some distance away from the long-promised "transparent" electoral process, but is headed in this direction.

PART II

COEXISTENCE

4 UNITED STATES– MEXICO FOREIGN RELATIONS

U nited States foreign policy after World War II focused especially on the nation's intense rivalry with the erstwhile Soviet Union, and on the direct implications of this struggle in Europe and much of the developing world. In general, U.S. officials—and the American public as well—viewed the world through the lens of superpower rivalry and judged each country on where it "stood" in relation to the competing ideologies of East and West.

   Given the incredible pace of world events in the late 1980s and early 1990s, it is hard to recall that as recently as the early 1980s, Ronald Reagan was attacking the Soviet Union as the "Evil Empire" and describing its dangerous and growing influence in Central America—warning in a later speech that "San Salvador is closer to Houston, Texas, than Houston is to Washington, D.C."[1]

As a consequence of America's preoccupation with the perceived menace from the Soviets and their satellites, U.S. relations with Mexico in the postwar period were more often than not characterized by 1) a general tendency to ignore the importance of economic and political relations with a country with which we share a 2,000-mile border and a pervasive and growing interdependence; and 2) a failure to understand that the dissimilar foreign-policy perspectives separating the U.S. and Mexico were based not on any Mexican affinity for the leadership in the Kremlin, but on Mexico's deep historical roots and interests—which are both very distinct from those of the United States and an important part of the Mexican psyche.

In earlier chapters we took a detailed look at these historical roots and learned that they still loom large in the Mexican memory. In the 19th century, there was the U.S. role in the secession of Texas, along with the loss of half of Mexico's territory in the "War of the North American Invasion" and its aftermath (the Treaty of Guadalupe Hidalgo and the Gadsden Purchase). In the 20th century, Mexicans' image of their northern neighbor has been colored by the occupation of the port of Tampico by U.S. marines, the "punitive expedition" of Gen. John J. Pershing, and, more recently, U.S. intervention in such nearby countries as Guatemala, the Dominican Republic, Grenada, and Panama.

A MATTER OF PERSPECTIVE

Mexico's own history and experience have led the country to develop a foreign policy and a style of conducting diplomatic

---

[1] White House, May 9, 1984.

relations that are unlike those of the United States. These differences cause problems for both sides.

Mexicans explain that their foreign-policy goals are based on a respect for national sovereignty, territorial integrity, and the right to self-determination. One of the linchpins of this policy is the Estrada Doctrine, named for former Mexican foreign minister Genaro Estrada, who in 1930 announced that Mexico's policy of non-intervention compelled it automatically to recognize other *de facto* governments regardless of their ideological position. This is a policy Mexico has followed with very few exceptions: A staunch supporter of the Spanish Republic, Mexico never recognized the Franco regime in Spain. Also, in solidarity with the Sandinistas in Nicaragua, President López Portillo broke relations with the Somoza government in 1971. In general, Mexico opposes intervention and, in the United Nations and other forums, supports the development of instruments of international law and multilateral political and economic negotiations.

American foreign-policy deliberations are often highly charged and very public, involving the Congress, the administration, the media, special interest groups, and the general citizenry (the Gulf War debate is a good recent example). But in Mexico foreign policy is generally made and executed quietly by the president and his team, advice is given in private sessions, and public criticism in the media, though certainly there, is relatively muted. This system is changing, as evidenced by the growing role of opposition party members in an increasingly influential Mexican Congress and by better reporting of the PRD and PAN leadership's public activities. However, foreign-policy issues in Mexico are still significantly less debated in the public eye than they are in the U.S.

One aspect of Mexico's foreign-policy activity has undergone substantial change in the last few years. There is a new Mexican willingness to promote its interests by engaging in high-profile activities in Washington, D.C. By early 1992 President Salinas had almost tripled the size of the professional foreign-service staff, advised by a cadre of lobbyists and assisted by trade experts and other specialists, in the newly expanded Mexican embassy in Washington. In major cities around the U.S., more than 75 consular officers are promoting Mexican foreign-trade interests, attracting foreign investment, and joining with their Washington counterparts in lobbying for the early negotiation and passage of the North American Free Trade Agreement. The consuls are also charged with establishing a close relationship with the Mexican-American communities in their geographically defined districts, an initiative that has the personal blessing of President Salinas.

These activities are in stark contrast to the quiet, low-profile path followed by a succession of Mexican ambassadors to the U.S. over recent decades. Perhaps concerned about establishing a precedent for reciprocal U.S. activities in Mexico, diplomats stayed out of the limelight and confined their representational efforts to the State Department, a few other government agencies, and, discreetly, the U.S. Congress.

But on substantive issues, Mexico has had little difficulty in maintaining its foreign-policy principles against the temptation to side with the United States. For example, in 1962, Mexico— true to the Estrada Doctrine and its conception of sovereignty and self-determination—opposed the passage of the U.S.-supported resolution in the Organization of American States that expelled Cuba from membership, and was the only Latin American country that maintained diplomatic relations with Cuba in subsequent years. Mexico perservered on this course despite harsh official U.S. criticism; in time the issue faded away. Indeed, on occasion Mexico's close contacts with the Cubans actually facilitated such operations as the airlift of Cuban exiles, who were permitted to pass through Mexico on their way to the United States.

MEXICO AND THE WORLD

Not until the presidency of Adolfo López Mateos (1958–64) did a Mexican administration adopt an active and internationalist foreign policy. Although López Mateos was elected after a campaign filled with leftist rhetoric and with the strong support of former president Lázaro Cárdenas, Mexicans were nonetheless somewhat surprised when their new president immediately undertook state visits to such Third World luminaries as Tito in Yugoslavia, Nehru in India, and Sukarno in Indonesia.

More important, President López Mateos actively supported the negotiations that led to the Treaty for the De-Nuclearization of Latin America, or the Treaty of Tlatelolco, for which the chief Mexican negotiator, Alfonso García Robles, subsequently shared the Nobel Peace Prize. The treaty negotiations were the chief international initiative of the López Mateos administration. While based on a worthy ideal, however, the treaty was not of great practical value, in large part because the two major potential nuclear powers in Latin America—Argentina and Brazil— never ratified it.

Contributing to Mexico's difficulties with the U.S. during the López Mateos administration were sharp differences over breaking relations with Cuba, the Mexican condemnation of the Bay of Pigs invasion in April 1961, and, later, Mexican concern during the October 1962 Cuban missile crisis. But a truce of sorts was declared in the summer of 1962, when President and Mrs. John F. Kennedy made a historic visit to Mexico City and were greeted by an immense outpouring of popular adulation for "Jack and Jackie" at a number of public ceremonies. Kennedy marked the occasion of his visit by noting in a public statement that "geography has made us neighbors, tradition has made us friends, and economics has made us partners."

There came a brief respite from the international foreign-policy initiatives of López Mateos during the presidency of the quiet, retiring Gustavo Díaz Ordaz (1964–70), who nonetheless worked tirelessly for the success of the 1968 Summer Olympics held in Mexico City. Unfortunately, those games are best remembered today because of the tragic deaths at the hands of army troops at the Plaza of Tlatelolco. (See Chapter 3.)

While eschewing much foreign travel, Díaz Ordaz did meet on a few but not particularly memorable occasions with presidents Johnson and Nixon. His successor, Luis Echeverría Alvarez (1970–76), immediately embarked on a highly activist, Third World–oriented series of foreign-policy initiatives. One key reason for this feverish effort is obvious: Echeverría had served as minister of the interior in the previous administration, where as the head of security services he was responsible for the handling of the Tlatelolco massacre. His desire to restore his credentials with leftist Mexican students and intellectuals involved him in a search for a role as a Third World leader.

Echeverría undertook an exceptionally arduous international schedule, visiting many Third World countries as well as Moscow and Beijing. Closer ties and reciprocal visits with Cuba's Fidel Castro and Chile's Salvador Allende were also on the agenda. Mexican activities at the U.N. included successful efforts to seek General Assembly approval of the now-defunct Charter of Economic Rights and Duties of States, opposed by the U.S. and other developed countries, and Echeverría's ill-advised support for an Arab-sponsored resolution equating Zionism with racism. (The resolution was rescinded in 1991.)

At home, Echeverría pursued a protectionist economic policy. His increased regulation of foreign investment and statist activities (for example, the nationalization of the telephone system) deterred potential foreign investors. At the same time, the public-sector deficit began to soar as, in an effort to stem a growing tide of rural discontent, he undertook a system of subsidies on basic commodities (corn, rice, milk, cooking oil, etc.) and extended rural road systems and electrification projects.

Massive deficit spending caused inflation to grow from an average of 5 percent a year in the previous administration to a then unheard-of 20 percent during Echeverría's last two years in office. As the other side of the coin, Echeverría spearheaded a nationwide crackdown on splinter groups led by former students and teachers who were organizing nascent rural and urban guerrilla organizations. While it is not clear how serious the situation might otherwise have become, his prompt and muscular counter-terrorist campaign, involving a considerable part of the Mexican army, brought an end to these post-Tlatelolco would-be insurgencies (but not before a series of ugly incidents occurred—see Chapter 3).

Later, Echeverría, who had a personal friendship with Chile's socialist president, Salvador Allende, opened Mexican government offices and academic institutions to a wave of leftist exiles who fled Chile following Allende's overthrow and mysterious death in September 1973. The exiles included Allende's widow and other family members. While these advisors and intellectuals were the cause of some irritation to those Mexicans who felt themselves pushed aside, the Chileans nevertheless played at least a modest role in the formation of Mexican government policies in the last two years of the Echeverría administration.

There was considerable surprise when the outgoing president picked his aristocratic finance minister, José López Portillo, as his successor.[2] American officials, and indeed the Mexican public in general, believed that López Portillo would usher in

---

[2] The reader is advised not to take too seriously arcane analyses of the Mexican presidential selection process over the past half-century. The next president of Mexico is picked by what Mexicans call the *dedazo*—the pointed finger of the incumbent, who makes his decision based on a delicate combination of his personal preference, the advice of influential figures close to him, and the *realpolitik* of the day. Once the presidential successor is chosen (the *destape*, or uncovering) the formal process of "selection" by the PRI and jockeying for position by a bevy of aspiring politicians proceeds.

a sober, conservative administration in contrast to the international flamboyance of his predecessor. Representatives of international financial institutions such as the International Monetary Fund and the World Bank looked forward to working with López Portillo to undo some of the damage of Echeverría's unwise economic policies.

THE OIL BINGE

Unfortunately, it turned out that Mexico would have to wait another six years for an honest, effective administration interested in the kind of structural reform the Mexican economy and political system required. Soon after the beginning of López Portillo's term (1976–82), the existence of huge new Mexican petroleum reserves was announced.

To get the feel of the early, heady years of the López Portillo administration, it is necessary to go back for a moment to 1960, when Saudi Arabia, Iran, Iraq, Kuwait, and Venezuela formed the Organization of Petroleum Exporting Countries (OPEC). The original motives were quite understandable. Until then, major international oil companies in effect set the price they would pay for crude; the oil-exporting countries felt, correctly, that they could negotiate better with the companies by joining forces.

While OPEC was somewhat successful in negotiations with international oil companies (oil prices rose from about $1 per barrel in 1960 to $3 a barrel in 1973), its attempts to achieve a more significant increase in world prices through a cartel approach were not successful until an exceptional event—the Yom Kippur War of 1973, which pitted Egypt against Israel—galvanized anti-Western sentiment among the Arabs and catalyzed close cooperation within OPEC. Saudi Arabia in particular hoped that the "oil weapon" could be used to threaten the U.S. and dissuade it from supporting Israel.

The U.S., believing that OPEC would never unite behind a

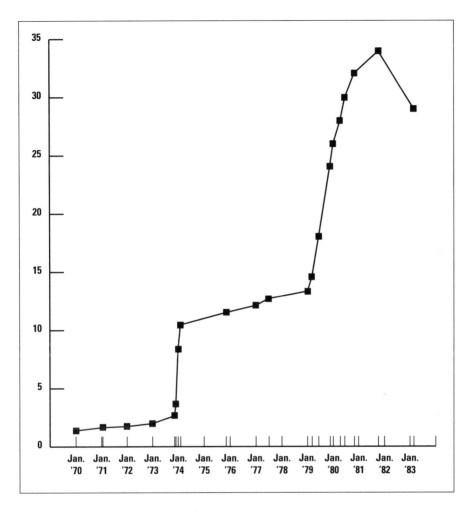

Figure 4.1
World Oil Prices (in U.S. dollars), 1970–83.

Saudi-led embargo on crude oil exports to the U.S., did not take the Saudi threat seriously. Thus the U.S. was caught by surprise when, on October 22, 1973, all the Arab countries of OPEC (that is, OPEC members excepting Iran and Venezuela), declared just such an embargo and cut their production immediately by 25 percent, creating a worldwide oil shortage.

Panic buying on world oil markets ensued, and prices went from $3 a barrel in early 1973 to $11 a barrel in early 1974, a one-year increase of almost 300 percent. While the OPEC embargo was a political failure—the U.S. continued to pursue a policy of strong support for Israel in the Middle East—the economic effects were considerable. Oil prices generally climbed steadily, reaching a peak of $37 a barrel in 1981 before dropping back to $31 in 1982 (and much further since).

The phenomenal increase in world oil prices had an equally phenomenal economic impact on Mexico. A net oil importer until 1973, Pemex quickly raised domestic prices for both crude oil and refined products, and began a rapid expansion program aimed at more intensive exploration and increasing production.

The exploration paid off during the early years of the López Portillo administration. In 1977 it was announced that Mexico's proven oil reserves were at least double the previously estimated 6 billion barrels. By 1980, proven reserve estimates had grown severalfold to an astounding 72 billion barrels.[3]

It was suddenly very easy for Mexico to negotiate multibillion-dollar development loans from big banks, which were for their part holding vast "petrodollar deposits" from OPEC beneficiaries of the oil boom. Thus López Portillo was able to ignore conventional advice from the IMF and others about the need to address galloping government overspending or the need for basic international trade and investment reforms; he proceeded to go full speed ahead on state-driven industrialization and a host of public-sector projects, many of them flawed by a level of official corruption perhaps unmatched in Mexican history before, or, certainly, since.

In 1978, the economy grew by an unstable 8.2 percent—a

---

[3] This estimate was scaled down in subsequent years. Pemex's 1992 estimate is that total oil reserves are about 45 billion barrels, and that all hydrocarbon reserves, i.e. oil and gas, amount to an equivalent of 65 billion barrels.

classic case of overheating, wherein external funds come pouring into a country and bring about inflation, overvaluation of the currency, and decreased international competitiveness. A staggering debt—to approach $100 billion by the end of the López Portillo administration in 1982—had been added to Mexico's future economic woes.

THE HAZING OF JIMMY CARTER

Meanwhile, López Portillo, elated by the oil bonanza, made little effort to respond cooperatively to President Jimmy Carter's genuine desire to improve ties. To the contrary, 1979 saw a low point in U.S.-Mexico relations. The problems began in February, when Carter journeyed to Mexico City for a meeting with López Portillo. The result was a series of controversial exchanges, including what Americans considered to be a rude lecture by López Portillo on past American sins and President Carter's infelicitous reference, in a public toast, to "Montezuma's revenge" (a term used to describe traveller's diarrhea). Even though the meeting ended with the announcement of some previously negotiated minor agreements and a mutual display of "friendship" at Carter's airport departure, the visit left both parties wary about the future.

When Carter returned to Washington, he decided to appoint a special coordinator with ambassadorial rank to oversee interagency relations with Mexico. Yet this well-intended effort merely exacerbated intergovernmental relations, as Mexicans were both suspicious of the move and uncertain about the chain of command. Was the "special coordinator" more important than the U.S. ambassador in Mexico? Or than the assistant secretary for inter-American affairs in the State Department? Why did he seem to Mexicans to be more concerned about U.S. business interests than in promoting good relations? These questions were never resolved, and the "special coordinator" idea was eventually abandoned.

The penultimate blow to the binational relationship in the ill-fated year of 1979 had its origins in Carter's efforts to accomplish a two-pronged policy in the troubled country of Nicaragua, long ruled by the dictator Anastasio Somoza. Popular resentment was building, and Somoza's days were numbered. The probable alternative to his rule, however, was hardly ideal. The Marxist-led Sandinistas were the most organized of the opposition elements, so it appeared likely that the Somoza dictatorship of the right would be replaced by a Cuban-style regime of the left. U.S. policy during this period sought to ease Somoza out but, at the same time, to encourage the creation of a ruling coalition of democratic parties and the Sandinistas. However, Mexico, in a move guaranteed to displease the U.S., supported the Sandinistas as the single most effective group in the struggle against Somoza. López Portillo seemed to delight in hosting the insurgent Sandinista *comandantes,* even providing them with the use of his personal aircraft.

But the worst was yet to come. In a series of personal telephone conversations, López Portillo had given his word to Carter that Mexico would provide medical asylum to the recently deposed and now ailing Shah of Iran. The U.S. proceeded on this assurance, only to be informed at a critical moment that Mexico was withdrawing its offer to the Shah. For all practical purposes this act severed personal relations between Carter, who described himself as outraged, and the Mexican president. It was no help when López Portillo made a triumphal visit to Nicaragua in 1980 after the Sandinistas seized power and took the opportunity to do a little more *yanqui*-bashing.

In any case, economic aspects of the two countries' relations began to have more salience in the latter part of López Portillo's term. The oil boom had by this time driven the Mexican economy into a red heat, generating substantial borrowing (more than $40 billion from U.S. and other foreign banks) and rapid growth of imports of capital goods in an effort to stimulate manufacturing and diversify exports away from oil dependency.

Then came the oil bust of the early 1980s. A rapid deterioration in Mexico's balance of payments, and in its ability to pay interest on its debts, followed. The situation came to a head with the dramatic Washington negotiations in August 1982, which rescued Mexico (and the world's financial markets) from the brink of disaster. (See Chapter 3.)

SOBERING UP

López Portillo's successor, Miguel de la Madrid (1982–88), preoccupied by the vast task of achieving domestic economic stability and structural reform, undertook few international initiatives. De la Madrid did, however, play a very constructive role, along with President Oscar Arias of Costa Rica and other South and Central American leaders, in efforts aimed at resolving the Nicaraguan civil war and its destabilizing impact on the region. A four-nation "Contadora group" consisting of Mexico, Panama, Venezuela, and Colombia was formed in January 1983, when, at Mexico's initiative, the four countries' foreign ministers met on Panama's Contadora Island to look for solutions to the crisis. Over the next few years, they worked with their Central American neighbors—usually with foreign ministers, but at the presidential level as well—to advance the peace process in a number of ways, including the negotiation of an agreement to avoid incipient war between Honduras and Nicaragua.

When the United States invaded Grenada in October 1983, de la Madrid expressed "profound concern," but without using the rhetoric or the high profile that would have been employed by his immediate predecessors. Mexico joined in when the U.N. General Assembly voted, 108 to 9, to denounce the invasion, which the U.S. had justified with the explanation that it was protecting American lives and property. The U.S. also claimed that Grenada was becoming a Soviet-Cuban base, and pointed ominously to the construction of a new airport whose runway was reportedly too long merely for tourism purposes. Most Mexicans were not convinced, but were too caught up with their own economic problems to make a major issue of the affair.

The presidential campaign of Carlos Salinas de Gortari (1988–94) began inauspiciously, with a breakaway faction of the government's own party, the PRI (in this case led by Cuauhtémoc Cárdenas) challenging the PRI in a presidential election. For the first time in decades, the presidential electoral battle was a spirited one. The outcome was at once clear and in doubt. That is, it is clear that Salinas won a *plurality* of the vote over his two main opponents, Cárdenas and Manuel Clouthier of the PAN. What is in doubt is whether Salinas won a *majority* of the votes, as announced several days after the polls closed, with a reported 50.1 percent.

President Salinas may have come into office bearing the burden of a disputed election, but he soon established himself as a legitimate and forceful president of Mexico. His balanced show of strength in the early weeks of his term—apprehending the notorious head of the state oil agency's corrupt union, and arresting a leading financial figure embroiled in stock-exchange chicanery—showed the new president to be the decisive figure of the sort that Mexicans much admire as leaders.

This helped pave the way for economic and social reform programs that have had a dramatic and positive effect on Mexico's future prospects. As we have seen, these include opening and modernizing the Mexican economy, reducing inflation, initiating such social projects as the multibillion-dollar *Programa Nacional de Solidaridad* (PRONASOL) and privatizing inefficient state industries. There is no doubt that if presidential elections were held in 1992, Salinas would emerge with a clear majority over his PRD and PAN rivals.

Economic and social changes have moved ahead more briskly

than the political reforms President Salinas promised in his inaugural address, but since late 1991 the pace of political reform has also begun to speed up noticeably. The most visible change has been the willingness of the government (for which read President Salinas) to nullify questionable gubernatorial elections in which the PRI candidate had been declared victorious. By February 1992, three such elections—in the states of Guanajuato, San Luis Potosí, and Tabasco—had been in effect nullified, albeit after popular protests.

Critics were quick to claim that these actions were taken simply to keep negotations for the North America Free Trade Agreement (NAFTA) on track, which requires that Salinas maintain the credibility he enjoys in the U.S. and Canada. Yet the fact remains that the net result has been to move the political process in Mexico toward a greater sensitivity to popular will—to democratize it. Clearly, this growing pluralism is in the best interest of the United States, which has much to gain from a southern neighbor that enjoys the kind of long-term stability only a pluralistic society can, in the end, provide.

In any case, it appears that the 1990s will not be a rerun of the intense foreign-policy differences of the 1980s, during which the U.S. and Mexico diverged radically on such issues as Central America, Grenada, and Panama. This in turn will undoubtedly fuel cooperation on NAFTA and other economic relations, migration, control of narcotics trafficking, the environment and transboundary resources, as well as honing each country's perceptions of the other's changing tastes, culture, and values.

5 DRUGS, RIVERS, AND DOLPHINS: STRIKING A BALANCE

Three concrete aspects of the complex relationship between Mexico and the United States rate a closer look: The first is the troubling drug trafficking issue, presented in historical perspective. Second is the International Boundary and Water Commission (IBWC), an institution that has been very successful in resolving a number of border and transboundary resource problems. Finally, recent developments in an environmental dispute provide a clear example of the complex and growing linkage between ecological concerns and international trade agreements—the so-called "dolphin issue."

DRUG TRAFFICKING

The issue of illegal traffic in drugs is an old one in the history of the United States and Mexico, and has had a cyclical character, from bitter disputes to close cooperation, over the years. To some extent, these cycles reflect such external factors as the sharp growth of international drug cartels (e.g., the "French Connection" or the "Medellin Cartel") and the increasing difficulty, for governments, of controlling the burgeoning traffic. But other factors have been at work as well, including the lack of clear-cut policies by either country on narcotics control and a failure to agree on the proper balance, e.g., between education and law enforcement, for the eradication of narcotics trafficking.

While both countries want to eliminate drug trafficking and sales, they are often in disaccord about how to go about this laudable goal. For example, Mexican authorities, who hold that the root cause of the problem is unbridled consumption on American streets, call on the U.S. to spend much more on education and drug treatment programs. American policy, though it does provide some funds for education and treatment, puts greater emphasis on the interdiction of narcotics on their way to the U.S.—either at the source, or in countries on the drug trafficking route.

Mexico has a long and impressive history of anti-narcotics activities stretching from the *Campaña Antidroga* (anti-drug campaign) of 1948 right up to 1990 (the most recent year for which data are available), when Mexico spent more than $200 million—including about one-third of Mexico's national defense budget—on anti-drug activities. During 1990, Mexican authorities report, 8,000 acres of opium poppy fields and 10,000 acres of marijuana fields were destroyed; 1,500 pounds of heroin and a million pounds of marijuana were seized; 11,000 drug traffickers were arrested, with 5,000 convicted and 6,000 awaiting trial; and 41 policemen and soldiers were killed in the line of duty in battles with drug traffickers, bringing the total over the 1987–90 period to 105. Mexicans, who themselves do not as yet face a serious drug abuse problem, consider that these efforts merit praise rather than criticism and are outraged by some U.S. sources' disparagement of Mexico's drug efforts.

Meanwhile, the magnitude of the socially destructive world drug trade keeps on increasing—to an estimated $300 billion in 1988—bringing with it the corruption and violence with which it has always been associated. U.S. Drug Enforcement Agency figures show that illegal drug use has permeated American society, and that 25 million users—almost one American in ten— paid some $100 billion to drug dealers in 1989. A Congressional committee put the 1990 figure at $110 billion. The committee found that while demand for heroin and marijuana has remained fairly constant, there has been a continued increase in demand for cocaine in its various forms, especially "crack" cocaine, a street drug that has a devastating effect on young addicts and, tragically, on their newborn babies. Crack and other drugs are blamed by U.S. authorities for most of the one-a-day murders on the streets of Washington, D.C. in 1990.

The U.S. response to the drug crisis has been building over the past decade. Total national anti-narcotics outlays rose from $1.4 billion in 1981 to $10.5 billion in 1990. About 70 percent of the total goes to local law enforcement efforts and foreign inter- diction, with the remainder destined for such areas as education or rehabilitation programs.

The importance of Mexico in the overall drug enforcement effort is shown in another set of figures: About half the mari- juana and 40 percent of the heroin coming into the U.S. arrives from Mexico, where marijuana and poppy fields are extensive. Although coca leaves are not grown in Mexico, a considerable amount of cocaine is transshipped through Mexican territory— officials estimate this amount at some 300 tons per year. The fact of a largely unpatrolled (and unpatrollable) 2,000-mile border, the ineffectiveness of the bilateral interdiction program (despite the billions of dollars being spent on it), and poverty in Mexico (which makes growing and trafficking attractive) are all elements in this equation.

U.S.-Mexico cooperation in drug trafficking goes back to the early 1920s, when Mexican president Alvaro Obregón, citing his country's adherence to the 1912 International Opium Convention, issued a series of decree-laws banning opium trade. Later, Plutarco Elías Calles (1924–28) signed international agreements banning international trafficking in marijuana and heroin and pledged to enact domestic legislation controlling the production and distribution of dangerous drugs. Lázaro Cárdenas (1934–40) was urged by the U.S. and other foreign governments to follow up on his predecessor's pledges, but other events—such as the nationalization of the oil industry and private American-owned ranches—took center stage during his administration, and little progress was made in drug control discussions.

During World War II, the U.S. shifted gears and encouraged legal poppy growing and opium production in Mexico to serve the wartime medical needs of the military services. But by 1944 opium production was getting out of hand, particularly in Sinaloa and Sonora. It was clear that the need for morphine (derived from the opium poppy) for military hospitals had been overestimated, and current stockpiles of the drug were more than sufficient. The two countries signed an agreement to cut production and prohibit illegal shipments, which nevertheless continued, though on a fairly modest scale.

The drug issue receded during the 1950s, but re-emerged with a vengeance in the 1960s. A new, "turned-on" lifestyle in the United States was creating a vast demand for marijuana—and to a lesser degree, for heroin—and Mexican growers and dealers responded. The U.S. government began, on the one hand, supplying Mexico with aircraft, training, and equipment for drug interdiction, and on the other hand, exerting increasing diplomatic pressure on Mexico to redouble its efforts to destroy opium poppy and marijuana crops and to interdict illicit drugs.

The explosive outcome of this high-pressure diplomacy was

predictably counterproductive. "Operation Intercept," launched on September 21, 1969, by U.S. law enforcement authorities (who were, in turn, advised by a shadowy figure on President Nixon's staff named G. Gordon Liddy), was the largest narcotics border-search and seizure operation in history. "Operation Intercept" caught the Mexican government—and the U.S. State Department—by surprise, and soon created an immense amount of ill will on the part of thousands of innocent Mexicans (and Americans) who were blocked from crossing border points for protracted periods, during which every person and vehicle were meticulously searched.

The Mexican press was highly critical of the operation—especially after the roughing up of a Mexican consul by U.S. agents—and complained that it was more successful in harassing Mexicans than in stopping drug traffic. In fact, very small amounts of drugs were actually seized, as the word quickly spread among *contrabandistas* (smugglers), who simply rerouted their cargoes to more-remote parts of the porous border.

Within days after "Operation Intercept" was announced, an ad hoc U.S. government inter-agency committee, composed of State Department and other representatives more interested in cooperation than in confrontation, met and quickly came up with a plan that was both far more effective and, importantly, acceptable to the Mexicans. "Operation Cooperation," unveiled October 11, 1969, replaced "Operation Intercept" and brought U.S. and Mexican agencies together in joint operations designed to reduce drug smuggling. There followed fifteen years of relatively smooth collaboration, including the plant-destruction program "Operation Condor" in the 1970s as well as a number of successful interdiction efforts, many of them based on U.S. worldwide intelligence contacts.

Criticisms of Mexico's anti-drug efforts are often based not on the efforts themselves, but on the widespread charges of human-rights abuses and corruption that accompany them.

Federal anti-drug police, the subject of numerous complaints to Mexico's recently formed Human Rights Commission, were one of the causes of the subsequent abrupt change in command at the top of the Mexican anti-drug program. On October 15, 1990, President Salinas named the number-two official in the Interior Ministry, Jorge Carrillo Olea, to be Mexico's new "drug czar" (actually, general coordinator of investigations into drug trafficking). Carrillo Olea's predecessor, Javier Coello Trejo, had compiled a good record in increasing cocaine and marijuana seizures, but was considered insufficiently responsive to human-rights abuse charges.

Carrillo Olea enjoyed a second public-relations advantage over Coello Trejo: He was not involved in the anti-narcotics program at the time of the abduction, torture, and murder of Enrique Camarena, an American citizen who served as U.S. Drug Enforcement Agency representative at the American Consulate General in Guadalajara. This macabre crime, committed in Guadalajara in February 1985 with the alleged complicity of local Mexican policemen, was bitterly and publicly criticized by senior U.S. officials in Washington and Mexico City, and not only marked the nadir in the cycle of narcotics trafficking cooperation in the 1980s, but also made more difficult the ongoing negotiation of other pressing bilateral issues.

The fallout of the Camarena case continued into the early 1990s, in part because of the forcible pick-up and transfer to U.S. authorities of a Guadalajara physician who was allegedly deeply implicated in the prolonged torture of Camarena. Mexican authorities, noting that the DEA had arranged what amounted to a kidnapping by bounty hunters (a claim the DEA did not deny), insisted that the physician be returned to Mexico. U.S. attorneys are alleging, however, that on the basis of past international precedent the physician can be tried in a U.S. court no matter how he came into its jurisdiction. The matter went through the U.S. courts in 1991, and in early 1992 the U.S.

Supreme Court agreed to hear the case.

Mexico's new drug czar has been working to downplay the negative aspects of this affair. But as this book went to press, the U.S. Supreme Court ruled in favor of the DEA's actions in this case. The extent to which this will exacerbate the binational relationship in the narcotics trafficking field, and in general, remains to be seen. What is clear is that the Court's decision flies in the face of international legal standards and the comity of nations.

For both the United States and Mexico, as well as the rest of the world, the drug crisis is far from over, and it appears that the efforts of successive U.S. administrations and other governments around the world have had little success. Whether this is due to a lack of resources devoted to these efforts, poorly chosen priorities, or other factors, it is difficult to say.

Mexican critics, however, have a strong consensus opinion: They say the U.S. is putting too much emphasis on interdiction while allocating far too few resources into drug prevention programs, particularly in the cities. They ask that the U.S. undertake massive new education and rehabilitation programs to reduce the seemingly insatiable demand for illicit drugs, and they call for genuine cooperation rather than unilateral U.S. pressure—epitomized by Operation Intercept—in international efforts aimed at curbing drug trafficking.

Mexicans also point out that the U.S. could do more in its own often-sporadic and politically sensitive domestic eradication efforts; even though marijuana production is estimated to be the largest cash crop of Hawaii, Oregon, and California, American growers seem largely immune from the kinds of enforcement actions the U.S. expects of Mexican authorities.

Mexicans, who feel that U.S. politicians sometimes find it easier to blame foreigners rather than confront domestic problems, were particularly troubled by leaks out of Washington toward the end of the Reagan administration that drug interdiction might be turned over to the U.S. Defense Department, and the international drug cooperation program "militarized." Some Mexicans saw this as a threat to their borders, airspace, and sovereignty and were greatly relieved when the Bush administration did not follow through on this supposed initiative.

Whether our Mexican neighbors are right or wrong in their priorities and concerns, no one would deny that drug use in the U.S. is of crisis proportions and, in the absence of an effective prevention policy, has the makings of a national tragedy. Mexico has not yet felt the force of significant domestic drug abuse, but history suggests that producing and transshipping countries are likely to face it sooner or later—the number of Mexican addicts is already on the rise. Mexican diplomats in the U.S. express concern about the growth of drug abuse among Hispanic-Americans and indicate that they are contemplating an outreach program to discourage this behavior in Hispanic communities in the U.S. In any case, narcotics trafficking will continue to complicate U.S.-Mexico relations for many years to come.

THE INTERNATIONAL BOUNDARY AND WATER COMMISSION

No description of United States-Mexico relations would be complete without mention of the International Boundary and Water Commission (IBWC), a binational commission established as a permanent joint entity by a treaty signed between the United States and Mexico in 1889. The IBWC grew out of a mutual effort to survey the international boundary established by the Treaty of Guadalupe Hidalgo in 1848 and the Gadsden Purchase in 1853.[2]

---

[2] The Water Treaty of 1944, signed to resolve boundary water problems caused in part by naturally shifting river beds, gave the IBWC additional responsibilities as well as a name change—it had until then been called the International Boundary Commission.

Despite the traumatic events that led to its creation—namely Mexico's loss of half its territory (and the gain by the U.S. of one-third of its territory)—the IBWC has served with few exceptions as a model of international cooperation. Undoubtedly, one of the reasons for this is that the commission has been kept as apolitical as possible. Both the U.S. and Mexican commissioners are required by treaty to be civil engineers; their staffs are exclusively professional. Any policy guidance comes from their respective foreign ministries, i.e., Mexico's *Secretaría de Relaciones Exteriores*, and the U.S. Department of State.

Among the IBWC's successes has been its important technical contribution to the resolution of the Colorado River salinity dispute. The Colorado River is a major source of water for the southwest United States and northwest Mexico. A huge project to irrigate U.S. farmland was undertaken in the 1950s and completed in 1961. But the diversion of Colorado River water to irrigation and the subsequent drainage of that water—by now having passed through saline farmland—back into the Colorado caused salinity levels to rise in the 1960s. This rendered several thousand acres of Mexicali Valley land south of the border unusable, forcing hundreds of *campesinos* off the land. In following years, the IBWC worked out an arrangement, signed by both nations in 1973, to build a desalting facility and dispose of unwanted brine.

The IBWC is responsible for the operation of the Rio Grande and Colorado River water distribution systems and international dams that control floods, conserve water, and generate electricity along the Rio Grande. It played an important advisory role in the Chamizal Settlement of 1963, thereby resolving a century-old dispute triggered by a sudden shift in the 1860s of the Rio Grande, which marked the boundary between the two border cities: El Paso, Texas, and Ciudad Juárez, Mexico. Since the early 1980s, the IBWC has taken on responsibility for growing transboundary wastewater problems (in large part a legacy of the *maquiladora* boom; see Chapter 8), and other emerging environmental issues.

TRADE, ECOLOGY, AND DOLPHINS

Over many decades, Americans have developed a great fondness for tuna, as evidenced by the growth of imports from some 30 countries—from 290 million pounds in 1960 to 990 million pounds in 1990. But these rapidly growing imports and the related dramatic increase in tuna fishing in international and domestic waters have a serious ecological downside. Dolphins, a marine mammal protected by U.S. legislation, are often found swimming in the same Pacific waters as yellowfin tuna. They are trapped and die—usually by drowning—in fishermen's nets. A 1972 federal law required American fishermen to adopt techniques that would limit dolphin deaths to 20,000 per year, and an amendment in 1988 banned imports from foreign countries that did not meet this domestic standard. After a two-year delay, the U.S. Department of Commerce in 1990 issued a ruling barring tuna imports from Mexico and other countries found to have higher percentage levels of dolphin deaths than those mandated for domestic fishing fleets.

This action led, in 1991, to something new in international relations: a resort to trade mechanisms to resolve an environmental issue. Mexico, a new member of the General Agreement on Tariffs and Trade, appealed the U.S. dolphin regulation to a GATT trade panel. In a precedent-setting ruling in Mexico's favor, the panel stated that no nation has the right to extend its environmental standards to international waters or foreign shores, and that imposition of such standards is an illegal restraint to international trade. While not denigrating the importance of preserving marine mammals, the GATT panel made the point that if it had ruled otherwise, countries could arbitrarily pass "environmental" laws that were in fact designed as non-

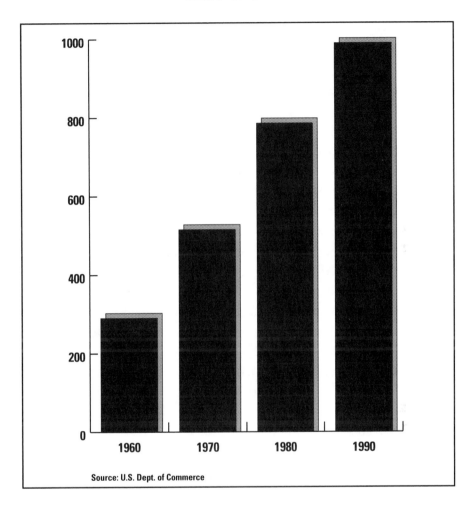

Figure 5.1
U.S. Tuna Imports from Mexico (in millions of pounds).

tariff barriers to trade. The panel thus concluded in effect that trade restrictions were an inappropriate tool for dealing with ecological problems, however meritorious.

Sensitive to the concerns of U.S. environmentalists and hoping to speed passage of the North American Free Trade Agreement (See Chapter 8), Mexico offered to negotiate the question of

tuna exports to the U.S. rather than insist on immediate implementation of the GATT decision. But these talks were disrupted
by a legal bombshell. On January 9, 1992, a judge of the Federal
District Court of San Francisco, acting on a complaint from environmental organizations, ruled that Mexico and two other
nations were in violation of the Marine Mammals Protection
Act. The judge forbade imports, direct or via third countries,
from Mexico, Venezuela, and Vanuatu, a tiny South Pacific island
country. Industry sources have estimated that this ruling, if it
stands up to appeal, would bar about half the tuna the U.S.
imports each year and would almost certainly push prices up-
ward. In any case, the judge's decision has had a chilling effect
on ongoing U.S.-Mexico negotiations over the dolphin issue.

To be sure, environmental issues are critical in today's world,
but the question remains as to whether the GATT is the appro-
priate mechanism for solving environmental questions. Insert-
ing environmental issues directly into the already very sensitive
GATT negotiations now in progress could very well delay or
even defeat the shared goal of an international regime of freer
and fairer trade—something that the world economy very much
needs, and soon.

THREE CONCRETE RECOMMENDATIONS

I have three concrete recommendations to improve the management of economic, political, and social relations among the three
countries of North America. The first, which I have been urging
for years, is very simple, but apparently troubling to bureau-
crats. For reasons best known to some long-defunct State Department administrator, the affairs of North America are now
handled in a curiously archaic way. Mexico is the responsibility
of a third-level official in the Bureau of Inter-American Affairs,
while Canada falls under a second-level official in—the Bureau
of European Affairs! As can be readily imagined, this makes it

difficult to focus on the barrage of emerging and vitally important North American issues that will affect the United States and its northern and southern neighbors in a growing interdependent way into the next century.

The solution: Create a Bureau of North American Affairs in the U.S. Department of State, headed by an assistant secretary who would be the senior U.S. government official coordinating North American affairs. She or he would be served by two principal deputy assistant secretaries for Canada and Mexico, respectively, and supported by existing State Department staffers, who would simply be transferred to the new bureau from their present assignments. No additional personnel would be required; but the result, in my opinion, based on more than twenty years' service in the State Department and abroad, would be a vast improvement in the way Washington looks at and deals with its closest neighbors, both of whom must rank as among the most important countries to the U.S. in a new, global era.

My second recommendation is to create a high-level public/private-sector commission, composed of government, labor, industry, media and other leaders from Canada, the U.S., and Mexico, which would meet twice a year for ongoing policy discussions about economic, political, and social issues affecting the entire North American continent. A small professional staff of policy research specialists would assist in preparing discussion papers prior to these meetings, and would deliver follow-up reports to the three governments and private-sector leaders.

A third, and related, recommendation would deal with the fact that there is far too little interplay of ideas among the members and key staff of the Canadian Parliament, the U.S. Congress, and the Mexican Congress. The result has been a long series of misperceptions and missed opportunities. While there is a history of "inter-parliamentary" relations going back at least as far as 1961, it is a far from satisfactory one; a new trinational mechanism that brought North American parliamentarians and their staff together with academic and other experts on a regular basis, with meetings held in all three countries by rotation, would be extremely useful. Long-term issues of vital interest to all three countries—including but by no means limited to such areas as trade and finance, investment, the environment, energy, education and culture, and migration—could be among the first to be studied. There is really no reason not to begin at once.

6 "Controlling" Migration

The border between the United States and Mexico divides and unites. It divides, because it marks the beginning and the end of our national identities, which we want to preserve. It unites, because we realize that only by learning to reach across it and working together can we pursue happiness with equality and freedom.

❧ Jorge Bustamante

Not only is America truly a nation of immigrants, but for the first century of its existence this country saw little need to control immigration. By and large, foreigners arrived on U.S. shores and entered into its economic life and civil society with a minimum of red tape. It was not until 1882, with the passage of the infamous Chinese Exclusion Act, that Congress made its first effort to limit the influx. This law not only prohibited Chinese immigration, but declared *ex post facto* that resident Chinese were to be stripped of their right to citizenship and deported.

That ominous harbinger was followed in 1921 by universally applicable immigration-control legislation aimed primarily at immigrants from Southern and Eastern Europe. This was accomplished by restricting the number of entrants from each foreign nation according to the frequency with which that nation already figured into the ancestry of America's resident population, as alleged under the 1920 census—a method heavily favoring Northern Europeans. Subsequent legislation refined the control process to take into account such factors as family reunification, the U.S. economy's need for skilled laborers, and a recognition of the growing problem of political refugees.

THE U.S.-MEXICO DIMENSION

Mexican emigration to the United States has been a factor in the two nations' relations for more than a century. In fact, since the times of the Texas Secession and the Mexican War, there has been a net *increase* in the Mexican population of U.S. border states. In the 1890s, for example, increasing numbers of Mexicans emigrated to Texas and, to a lesser degree, to New Mexico, Arizona, and California in search of social stability, better education for their children, and improved economic opportunities. This movement accelerated during the decade of the Mexican Revolution (1910–20) as hundreds of thousands of Mexican citizens, many of them from the upper social classes, fled the violence of the times and sought refuge in the U.S. Nor were their peregrinations confined to the border states; Mexican immigrant communities began to develop in several major industrial cities, especially Chicago.

These influxes, at least up to 1920, were seldom accompanied by significant social friction, and with few exceptions the Mexican immigrants tended to find jobs and acceptance in their communities. But gradually, conservative groups in the United States began to grumble about "losing control of our borders." As a result of such complaints from constituents, Congress created the U.S. Border Patrol in 1924, and organized efforts were undertaken for the first time to arrest and deport "illegal Mexicans," sometimes disparagingly called "wetbacks" (*mojados*, in Spanish) because some of them gained entry to the U.S. by wading or swimming across the Rio Grande.

When the Great Depression hit the United States (and the world) in 1930, there were an estimated one million undocumented Mexican men, women, and children living in the United States. Overreacting to the shrinking job market, the U.S. began a "voluntary repatriation" program which eventually sent some 300,000 Mexicans back to their country. Although its effect on combatting the social effects of the U.S. depression was small, this program succeeded in exacerbating economic problems in Mexico, adding to already serious unemployment and fueling anti-U.S. feelings there.

The end of the depression and the outbreak of World War II changed the migrant picture dramatically. Far from discouraging Mexican workers, the U.S. Government and Mexico negotiated in 1942 a *bracero* (laborer) agreement that brought more than a quarter-million farm and transportation industry workers to the U.S. with a guarantee of decent wages, health care, and working conditions.

The end of the first *bracero* program in 1947 (similar programs were initiated from time to time until 1964) ushered in a period of some two decades of benign neglect on the part of U.S. authorities. Border Patrol activities were predictable, enforcement was spotty, and millions of undocumented Mexican workers—

usually unaccompanied young males—came and went, pushed by unfavorable economic conditions in their communities in Mexico and pulled by the greater job opportunities in a generally expanding U.S. economy.

The typical undocumented worker of those days left his family behind in a small village in central or southern Mexico, to which he returned regularly. After a few years in the U.S., during which he acquired savings and a knowledge of the world outside rural Mexico, this worker found himself a well-respected and even revered member of his home community, and often bought property and settled down there after fifteen or twenty years' work in the U.S.

This description of the undocumented worker has changed over the past twenty years. Today, he or she (by 1991, almost half of all undocumented border crossings were by women) is better educated, almost certainly literate, and leaving a job in Mexico. This reflects changing internal migration patterns in Mexico. As *campesinos* leave the countryside and seek work in towns or cities, they are apt to replace workers who have acquired education and skills and only then emigrated to the U.S. In time, after having acquired job skills and a better understanding of the dynamics of the emigration process, the former *campesinos* may themselves join the flow. Alternatively, the *campesino* who is more adventurous and perhaps even a leader in his rural community may go directly to a "home" community in the U.S., populated by friends and relatives from his particular region of rural Mexico. These networks of *gente de confianza*— people in whom he has confidence—take him to a friendly and welcoming neighborhood in, say, California, Texas, or Illinois where he is made to feel at home, is given employment, and begins what is likely to become a permanent residence.

In any case, the skill and educational level of the typical Mexican worker coming to the U.S. has risen markedly in recent years. In addition, more women and children are joining the immigration steam each year, suggesting that residence in the U.S. might be more permanent in nature. Both of these phenomena are believed to have been in part the result of the Mexican economic crisis (1982–85) described in a previous chapter.

While in the past there was an unspoken feeling in Mexico that emigration to the U.S. was a safety valve releasing the social tensions of unemployment, many Mexicans now see unmanaged emigration as a net economic and social loss for their country. They are rightly, and increasingly, concerned about the loss of young, educated, skilled men and women to productive jobs in the United States, where they contribute to the U.S. rather than the Mexican economy. It is estimated that more than 25 percent of the workforce in California's high-tech Silicon Valley are undocumented Mexicans—who also, of course, play important roles in construction, agriculture, food processing, and service industries such as hotels and restaurants. It is hoped in Mexico that the successful conclusion of a North American Free Trade Agreement will enhance Mexican industry and create employment through increased foreign and domestic private direct investment, thereby keeping workers at home.

For the United States, however, the benefits of Mexican immigration are immense and will increase in the 1990s and beyond. Demographic patterns of the United States indicate that we are entering an era of growing labor scarcity. The U.S. Census Bureau reports that a decreasing birth rate since the middle of the 1960s has produced a declining and increasingly "geriatric" U.S.-born work force. According to the Bureau, annual growth of the U.S. work force has declined from 5 percent in the 1970s to an estimated 1.5 percent in the 1990s. U.S. economic growth in the last years of this century and on into the next can thus be supported only by external supplies of entry-level workers. Our neighbor to the south—a "pediatric society"—has an excess supply, with an estimated 1.1 million young Mexicans coming into the job pool each year. These potential workers find only about half that number of new jobs open to them, even in a growing Mexican economy. In any case, a young and able Mexican worker can earn in an hour in the U.S. what a day's work at a similar job would bring him or her in Mexico! That 8-to-1 or greater wage differential exerts a powerful attraction on mobile, usually young, Mexicans. This is fortunate, for, without this needed supply of youthful labor in the service, light-industrial, and other sectors, many businesses in the U.S. would close—with a consequent loss of jobs for U.S.-born as well as foreign-born employees.

While no one disputes the sovereign right of the United States to bar illegal workers, these economic considerations would seem to suggest that a solution to the problem be sought that is based on our real best interests. For example, over the next 20 years, an estimated 30 million new jobs will be created in the U.S.—10 million in California alone—most of which will be at entry-level in the service, information, and other sectors. Given our demographics, only a fraction of these jobs could possibly be filled from domestic sources. Where are many of the new workers coming from? The most reasonable response: from Mexico.

This will happen despite official U.S. law enforcement policies. Time and again, the U.S. government has spent substantial sums to build a few miles of fences or other barriers to Mexican emigration, only to have them skirted (or dug under!) in a matter of hours or days. The sooner we learn that these efforts are essentially a waste of the taxpayer's money, the better. It is highly unlikely that the American public would ever stand for a virtual militarization of the entire border, which would require thousands of troops and uncounted millions of dollars to noticeably affect the migration flow.

More disturbingly, as long as such border crossings are illegal, great suffering and even physical harm is visited upon undocumented workers by *coyotes*, criminals who prey on them

Figure 6.1
For young and old alike, the chain-link boundary line
separating Nogales, Arizona, from Nogales, Sonora,
is little more than a daily inconvenience.

while ostensibly offering them safe passage across the international border. Anyone who has seen the moving film *El Norte* is aware of this situation. But as long as jobs are opening up, in California or elsewhere in the U.S., young Mexicans will be there to claim them. The real challenge for policymakers is to learn how to make migration work to both countries' benefit.

THE NUMBERS GAME

The most often asked questions concerning Mexican immigration are: How many legal and illegal persons of Mexican origin are there now in the United States, and how many are added each year? While the questions are simple, they are hard to answer. It is estimated that when 1990 census data are analyzed and corrected, they will show that of the 13 million or so people of Mexican origin now living in the United States, perhaps 9 million are U.S.-born. Of the approximately 4 million Mexican-born residents, about 3.5 million are legal immigrants and some half-million are undocumented workers, both transient and permanent. Between 70,000 and 80,000 new legal immigrants enter the U.S. from Mexico each year—and, as roughly estimated, at least that number of undocumented workers (on a net basis).

These numbers, which are tentative at best, fluctuate with the millions of border crossings that take place in *both* directions every year (which are, in turn, a function of prevailing economic conditions), the registration of previously undocumented workers under the amnesty provisions of the Immigration Reform and Control Act of 1986 (about 2.3 million so far), and numerous other factors.

One message that often gets lost in the shuffle, however, is that the vast majority of Mexican-Americans are here legally. The constant focus on illegal immigrants tends to cause us to lose sight of this important fact, and to fail to recognize the immense richness of the cultural diversity, creative imagination, and productivity that Hispanics are bringing to our shared society.

THE U.S. DEBATE ON IMMIGRATION REFORM: 1970–86

Perhaps the greatest debate over illegal immigration from Mexico has taken place within the United States itself. But fallout from that debate frequently spills over the border, especially when some opponents of immigration make highly intemperate arguments that sound suspiciously racist to the admittedly sensitive Mexican ear.

After the end of the last *bracero* program in 1964, the growing conflict between the need for workers and the desire to "protect the borders" forced U.S. lawmakers to take a new look at the broad field of immigration and American society. Following a decade of debate which failed to produce any Congressional consensus on new legislation, President Carter appointed a Select Commission on Immigration in 1978 and named Father Theodore Hesburgh, president of Notre Dame University and a well-respected national figure, to head it.

The commission's report, issued in 1981, set the broad outlines for immigration reform, including amnesty and the imposition of employer sanctions, but discarded certain controversial suggestions. For example, a tamper-proof national identity card, which among other things would provide immediate validation of residence or citizenship status, was opposed by many civil libertarians—despite the fact that, as proponents of the card noted, many other major democracies around the world require such identification from their citizens and permanent residents, apparently without any staggering deprivation of their civil rights. In any case, the commission eventually abandoned the national identity card idea.

THE IMMIGRATION REFORM AND CONTROL ACT OF 1986

There followed a five-year struggle in the Congress to get immigration-reform legislation passed. Over time, the bill took on the coloration of special interests: more enforcement for the Border Patrol to satisfy conservatives; broader amnesty provisions to make liberals happy; weakened rules for employers to appeal to business and industry interests; special programs for agricultural workers to appease agribusiness; etc., etc.. Finally in 1986, after intense debate and persistent efforts by Sen. Alan Simpson (a fan of the Border Patrol) and Reps. Romano Mazzoli and Peter Rodino, a catch-all law was passed.

During the months preceding its passage, both supporters and detractors had declared the bill dead, but it was resurrected at the last moment—in part so that senators and congressmen could return to their constituencies in an election year with a claim to have done something about an immigration "problem" that (shades of the 1920s) was again said to be threatening the control of our borders. In signing the bill into law on November 6, 1986, President Reagan suggested that "future generations of Americans will be thankful for our efforts to humanely regain control of our borders. . . . In the past 35 years our nation has been increasingly affected by illegal immigration. . . . This legislation takes a major step toward meeting this challenge to our sovereignty." As we shall see, these remarks have proven to be overly optimistic.

The new law, known by its acronym IRCA (for Immigration Reform and Control Act), departed from all previous immigration legislation in at least two important respects. For one thing, it recognized that the 2,000-mile border between the U.S. and Mexico was so porous that it was virtually impossible for law enforcement agencies alone to significantly reduce illegal immigration; the bill instead put the onus on employers by including a provision that made it illegal in most cases to knowingly hire an undocumented worker.

Until the passage of IRCA, a curious anomaly had existed: while it was illegal for undocumented immigrants to come to the U.S. for work, it was not illegal for employers to hire them! By requiring employers to verify the immigration status of new employees under pain of civil and criminal penalties, IRCA seemed initially to be eliminating this anomaly. But in practice, this provision has turned out to be almost impossible to enforce. Employers merely have to certify that they have viewed the proof of legal residence presented by the worker when he or she was hired, and were satisfied that the credentials appeared genuine. There is no requirement that the employer take any further steps to verify the authenticity of the documentation offered. And, of course, the employer cannot retain the documents. So when Immigration and Naturalization Service inspectors arrive at a job site, they see only a company record that claims: "Yes, Juan Gómez appeared on a certain date and showed documentation, which seemed genuine." Needless to say, such procedures constitute an invitation to evasion, ranging from a less-than-careful scrutiny of documents to the sharing of documents among illegal workers, forged documents (readily available in any major U.S. city for a modest price), etc. It is not surprising, then, that IRCA's "employer sanctions" provisions have proven ineffective.

A second major way in which IRCA differed from all previous immigration legislation was that it provided for amnesty, and eventual permanent residence, to illegal aliens who have resided continuously in the U.S. since January 1982. While there have been some hitches—in some cases forged documents, in others the inability of some genuinely eligible candidates to prove their case—in general the amnesty program has been a success, as some 2.3 million previously undocumented immigrants have been able to regularize their status.

A third provision of IRCA—a reward to Senator Simpson—was not pathbreaking; it simply reinforced the Border Patrol budget—though, as it turns out, with limited long-term effect. Still other provisions attempted to ensure the civil rights of resident aliens and U.S. citizens of Hispanic origin and provided Federal support for local welfare programs serving newly amnestied clients. Finally, as a reflection of the serious concerns of U.S. agribusiness, the bill gave special preference to seasonal agricultural workers from Mexico.

CURRENT MIGRATION FLOWS

It is clear from the legislative record that the passage of IRCA reflected, in large part, an understandable desire on the part of the legislative and executive branches of the government to reassure the American electorate they were acting together to "regain control of our borders." Whatever good IRCA may have accomplished—for example, the humanitarian aspect of the amnesty provisions—it does not appear over time to have slowed the number of undocumented workers entering the U.S. from Mexico, although in the months immediately after the law's passage, a decline in attempted entries was noted. Illegal immigration dipped slightly in late 1986 and early 1987, but it did not take long for Mexican workers to discover that there were still jobs to be found north of the border, as well as easy ways to present "proof" of legal residence. By 1988 flows were back to pre-1986 levels.

While the northward flow does vary, it appears to do so independently of IRCA and border-control procedures, and mainly in response to economic conditions. For example, during the Mexican economic "boom" of 1980–82, which coincided with a recession in the U.S., illegal immigration to the U.S. declined modestly, only to pick up again in the years 1982–85, which were marked by severe economic crisis in Mexico and economic recovery in the U.S.

The policy implications are obvious: We should stop focusing on immigration as primarily a law enforcement issue and recognize that long-term solutions can be found only in the context of the U.S. and Mexico's rapidly growing economic and social interdependence. Perhaps the complex negotiations underway among Mexicans, Americans, and Canadians on the North America Free Trade Agreement will create an atmosphere conducive to such an attitude change. Certainly, labor and migration issues, while not direct free-trade concerns, are closely related. Discussions parallel to the ongoing free-trade talks might be an ideal place to begin to "decriminalize" migration and consider more seriously the underlying economic and social forces instead, and to devise a cooperative trinational program to deal effectively with North American labor flows.

To summarize: Mexican immigration to the United States in the 1990s has assumed a combination of familiar and newly emerging patterns. While significant numbers of young males continue to work in the U.S. agricultural sector, returning to Mexico when the season ends, they are rapidly becoming outnumbered by immigrants who intend to stay permanently. In both cases, an increase in "pull factors" drawing new workers can be expected as the U.S. comes out of its recession during 1992–93 and labor demand in almost all sectors rises. Migration flows appear to be sensitive to economic conditions in both countries, but particularly to those in the United States.

While in theory the improvement in Mexico's economy achieved during recent years should have reduced "push" factors in Mexico, there is little evidence at present that the willingness of Mexican workers to emigrate has diminished. This is only one reason why Mexican and U.S. policymakers should be working together to develop a joint migration policy that will be in the best interest of U.S. employers and the Mexican workers who emigrate to the U.S. Such a policy might involve, for example, an expansion of temporary worker visas to meet seasonal needs in agricultural areas, as well as closer supervision of how immigrant workers are paid, housed, and treated.

Less likely to be successful—though an inviting prospect to many with a pragmatic frame of mind—is retaining the *status quo*: that is, keeping on the books laws such as IRCA that restrict undocumented workers *de jure*, while relying *de facto* on undocumented workers to contribute importantly to America's economic progress. An integral part of this approach is the exploitation by employers of undocumented workers, who will be able to enjoy the full benefits of our open society only when their status is legalized. How this latter can be accomplished—whether by an expanded guest worker program, by a sharp increase in immigration quotas, or in some other way—should be the subject of urgent and intensive discussions involving both public- and private-sector policy experts in Mexico, the U.S., and, for that matter, Canada.

THREE RED HERRINGS: WORKER DISPLACEMENT, WELFARE ABUSE, AND CULTURAL SEPARATISM

Do immigrants abuse welfare programs and create a problem for taxpayers? Do they displace American workers? Do they refuse to learn English or to integrate into American society? These questions about Mexican migration are often advanced, and continue to be so even though they have been answered convincingly by academic studies. (See the Reader's Guide for Chapter 6 at the end of this volume.)

It is sad to observe some American politicians putting forward claims, often overtly racist in tone, that foreigners are a drag on the economy or abuse the welfare system. That there is no factual basis for these charges, and that all reputable research reports to the contrary, does not seem to faze these opportunists as they go for a cheap shot. A number of studies in the field show that immigrants do not in general abuse welfare programs—indeed, they are often afraid to seek the benefits to which they are entitled. Neither do immigrants as a rule directly displace American workers; in fact, their contributions to a firm, by keeping it competitive, often permit it to continue to hire American workers.

The most complex of the three questions asked above addresses sensitive matters: how members of the immigrant culture relate to mainstream American society, and the meaning and even the desirability of "assimilation" of recently arrived members of American society, whether legal or undocumented.

An active part of the U.S.-born population takes an "English-only" approach to education, voting, and other civil events.[1] Their feeling is that immigrants should renounce their native languages and cultures and conform to "American" norms of speech and behavior. These are often people who remember, or misremember, the good old days of the "melting pot," when, it is recalled, immigrants came from many lands and rapidly assimilated into the American mainstream. Never mind that a close look at the history of Irish, Italian, Jewish, Latin American, Asian, and other immigrants to the United States over the past two centuries does not support the notion of seamless fusion; the nostalgia continues, and calls for conformity on immigrants' part to the ideals of the American Dream are heard.

But a majority of thoughtful opinion leaders today accept in principle the idea that cultural pluralism—as represented by the culture, tastes, and values of Mexican immigrants—is recasting America as an exciting mosaic, bringing a richness to the receiving communities that makes them better places to live. That is, the debate is over the *degree* of cultural pluralism compatible with full and equal participation of immigrants in the political process, the productive sectors of the economy, and civil society. Even if one hopes that Mexican-Americans will retain their original language (and, indeed, that more and more non-Spanish-speaking Americans will learn it!), it is still necessary that newcomers learn English quickly in order to compete in the economy and contribute to the benefit of American society.

---

[1] For example, an "English-Only" proposition was approved by California voters on November 4, 1986, and became Article III, Section 6 of the California State Constitution law. Article III, Section 6 of the California Constitution states *inter alia* that "English is the common language of the people of California. This section is intended to preserve, protect, and strengthen the English language, and not to supersede any of the rights guaranteed to the people by this Constitution."

"Bilingual education" should really denote a process by which teachers use their students's knowledge of Spanish (or other first languages) to train them more readily and effectively to read, write, and speak English. At the same time, public-school instruction in world history and cultures and foreign languages should be strengthened, with the goal of creating a bilingual— or multilingual—society able to meet the demands of an emerging global era.

Conformity is unenforceable, and pluralism is inevitable. Take California, for example, the majority of whose population will be of Hispanic ancestry within a decade or two into the new century. The real question is not one of enforced conformity vs. "permitting" cultural pluralism, but of how well we can accommodate a dramatic increase in cultural pluralism while maintaining the common goals that have made America, despite its imperfections, one of the world's greatest and most prosperous democracies. With the Cold War behind us, this is one of the most important challenges facing political leaders today.

But a major problem for policymakers—even after they recognize that immigration at foreseeable levels over the coming decades will result in considerable gains for all—will be to convince people still fearful of "losing control" that the real problems of drugs, crime, gangs, homelessness, and a declining education system do not have immigration as their source, tempting as that is to believe.

We have never really "controlled our borders" in the past, yet the country has thrived—both immigrants and natives alike. Historically, immigration policy (in practice if not in law) has rested on the firm economic fact that immigrant labor was needed in 19th- and 20th- century America. Such an influx of workers will be at least as necessary, maybe more so, in the 21st century, now only a few years away.

7 TOWARD AN ECONOMIC PARTNERSHIP

A s the 1990s began, notions about international relations that had been formed during the post–World War II period were starting to crumble. During the late 1980s, one after another old communist regime in East Europe fell, and the essential internal weakness of the Soviet Union—which was to disappear in 1992—became increasingly apparent. These momentous developments have shifted the attention of the United States from the international security issues of the bipolar nuclear world of the 1950s–80s to pressing global and regional economic issues—a move that has had favorable implications for U.S.-Mexico economic relations and for trade negotiations involving all of North America.

At the same time that world events, combined with

concerns about growing trade deficits and a sluggish economy, were turning America's attention to regional economic issues—for example, the negotiation of the U.S.-Canada Free Trade Agreement of January 1988—exactly the kind of economic policy reforms that were vitally needed to thrust Mexico successfully into the world economy were taking place under the leadership of Presidents Miguel de la Madrid and Carlos Salinas in Mexico.

As we have seen, the United States has played a persistent role in the development of Mexico's political economy, particularly since the time of the *porfiriato* (1876–1910). In general terms the economy, which suffered dramatically during the violent stages of the Revolution (1910–20), recovered only slowly afterward. The next 25 years were shaped by a world depression; the growing involvement of the state, exemplified by the nationalization of Mexico's oil industry in 1938; and World War II (1939–45).

World War II catalyzed a considerable degree of economic cooperation between the United States and Mexico. The U.S. bought Mexican raw materials for its war effort and used the *bracero* program to substitute Mexican laborers for American youth called to the military services. This cooperation continued during the postwar era, when Mexican leaders saw that the building by the state of a firm infrastructure and control of primary industries should be balanced by the development of a viable private sector and an expansion of foreign trade.

Unfortunately, Mexico fostered this private-sector growth by adopting a policy of import-substituting industrialization: The state erected stiff protectionist barriers to foreign imports in order to subsidize "infant" private industries. From 1950 until 1982, tariffs were increased whenever necessary to protect both private and state-controlled industries in what effectively became a closed Mexican economy. The resulting growth, while dramatic (output rose by an average of 6.5 percent annually during this period), was unsustainable in the long run.

A TWELVE-YEAR DECLINE IN RELATIONS BEGINS

Both Mexico's economic difficulties and its relations with the U.S. were exacerbated by the growing deficits and Third World rhetoric of the Echeverría administration (1968–74), which culminated in rampant capital flight and the devaluation of the peso by 60 percent. The López Portillo administration (1974–82) was the most disastrous since the Revolution; by its end, U.S.-Mexico relations were at a post-Revolutionary low. The Mexican economy went into a recession, then recovered powerfully but briefly during the heyday of the oil boom (1978–81). But the amassing of incredible new debt during that boom ended with the crash of 1982. During his final weeks in office, López Portillo nationalized the banking system, and the complete collapse of private-sector confidence in the Mexican political and economic scenes was ensured.

The 1982 crisis was a reflection of the weakness of the Mexican economy caused by overdependence on the import-substitution development model, which created a closed, noncompetitive economy vulnerable to external shocks. The collapse of world oil prices and rising international interest rates wreaked havoc on Mexico's foreign debt, which had reached historic highs during the brief "oil boom" years.

DE LA MADRID AND SALINAS EMBARK ON ECONOMIC AND POLITICAL REFORM

But with the advent of Miguel de la Madrid to the presidency in late 1982, U.S.-Mexico relations began what was to be a decade of dramatic improvement. The six-year term of President de la Madrid (1982–88) was divided almost evenly between:

1) *economic adjustments.* During his first three years in office, de la Madrid reduced inflationary pressures, stabilized the exchange rate at a level where Mexican exports were more competitive, limited government expenditures, and cut traditional

subsidies on basic foodstuffs.

2) *external economic reform*. Mexico joined the GATT; tariffs were sharply reduced to an average of only 7 percent, with a maximum tariff of 20 percent; the requirement that imports of foreign goods be subject to government licenses was all but eliminated; and an arrangement for resolving U.S.-Mexico trade disputes was created.

The adjustments and reforms of the de la Madrid administration resulted in important new world trade relationships. Ironically, these strides were facilitated by the very devastation of the López Portillo regime, as the Mexican people realized that twelve years of ideological rhetoric, nationalizations, and protectionism had brought them to disaster. They were now ready to try the sometimes bitter remedies of austerity and stabilization.

SALINAS EXPANDS INTERNAL REFORM, U.S. TRADE RELATIONS

All this set the stage for the radical opening of the Mexican economy during the Salinas administration (1988–94). Internal economic reform accelerated, relations with President Bush's administration improved, and the foreign debt was restructured. Encouraged by a growing U.S. economy in the early 1980s and by improving trade relations, Mexican industry shifted to an export-driven strategy, which was rewarded by a significant improve-ment in the composition and level of U.S.-Mexico trade balances.

As elsewhere in U.S.-Mexico relations, asymmetries abound in bilateral trade. In recent years the U.S. share of total Mexican trade (exports and imports) has risen from 65 percent to 75 percent; exports to the U.S. account for 14 percent of Mexico's GDP. In comparison, Mexico's share of total U.S. trade has risen from 5 percent to a mere 7 percent; exports to Mexico account for less than 1 percent of the huge American GDP. Still, the increase in trade has been a great plus for the Mexican economy. (See Fig. 7.1).

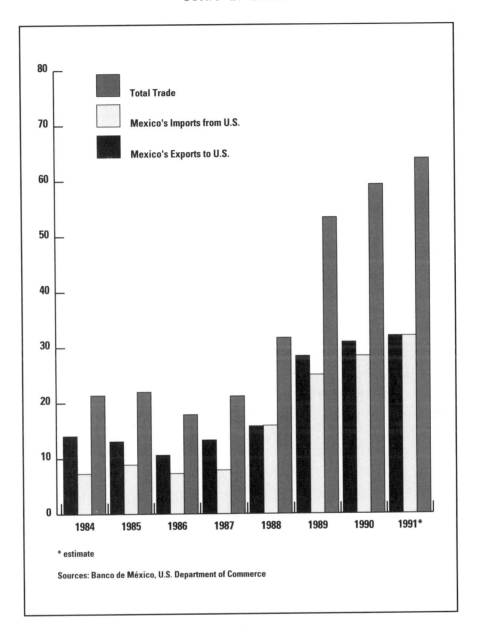

Figure 7.1
U.S.-Mexico Trade (in billions of U.S. dollars).

Moreover, the composition of trade has changed quite substantially. In the late 1970s and early 1980s, Mexican exports to the U.S. were dominated by petroleum, with crude-oil exports running strong until 1984, after which they began to decline. This decline, however, was accompanied by a significant increase in Mexico's exports of manufactured goods to the U.S., which increased threefold in the 1980s. Important Mexican exports now include machinery and transportation equipment, automotive parts, cement, steel, iron pipes, tiles, glass products, minerals, agricultural products, apparel, and shoes.

Meanwhile, as Mexico began to recover from the crisis of 1982, U.S. exports rose markedly, especially in the vital areas of capital goods, machinery and transportation equipment, and chemicals. Mexico's opening of its economy, accompanied by new private investment, created a growing demand for capital and intermediate goods. This demand has greatly stimulated U.S. exports in recent years, especially 1987–91, making Mexico the third-largest U.S. trading partner after Japan and Canada.

This growth in trade between the U.S. and Mexico is projected to continue, especially if the North American Free Trade Agreement (NAFTA) negotiations now in progress stay on track. Total bilateral trade—which amounted to $53 billion in 1989, $59 billion in 1990, and an estimated $64 billion in 1991—should reach $66 billion in 1992 and grow more rapidly thereafter, assuming the ratification of NAFTA and an even modestly improving U.S. economy. The U.S. had a small bilateral trade surplus in 1989, and a smaller one in 1990. Some experts predict a small Mexican surplus in the early 1990s, but by and large U.S.-Mexico trade should continue to be essentially in balance.

THE MEXICAN FOREIGN INVESTMENT BOOM

Foreign private direct investment has surged in Mexico in recent years (an influx of more than $11 billion during the 1989–91

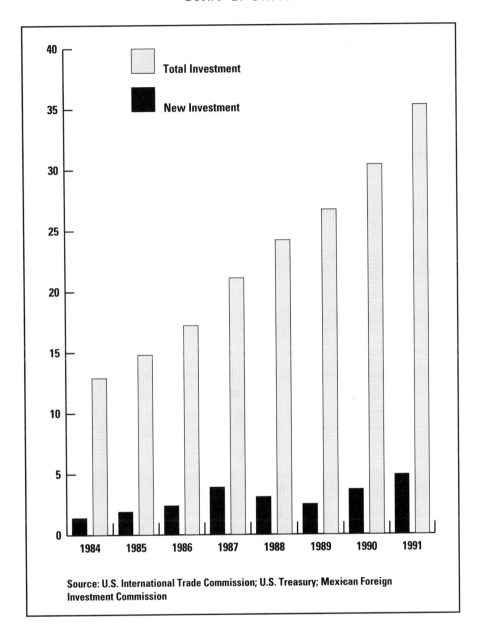

Source: U.S. International Trade Commission; U.S. Treasury; Mexican Foreign
Investment Commission

Figure 7.2
Foreign Direct Investment in Mexico
(in billions of U.S. dollars).

period), for a number of reasons.(See Fig. 7.2). President Salinas has reinterpreted Mexico's restrictive regulations to make foreign investment in Mexico more attractive. Just as important, his program for stability and growth has reduced inflation in Mexico from 30 percent in 1990 to 18 percent in 1991 and a projected 12 percent in 1992. Driven by a newly optimistic private sector, the economy is growing at a sustainable pace: 3.1 percent in 1989, 3.9 percent in 1990, 4.1 percent in 1991, and an estimated 4.2 percent in 1992. All these developments reinforce each other.

Even more advantageous, Mexico's economic growth encompasses a wide range of industries. Growth during 1991 was notable in transportation and communications (6.6 percent); manufacturing (4 percent); and tourism (6 percent). Notably lagging is the agricultural sector, which grew by only 2 percent in 1991 but is projected to pick up when several agricultural reforms, announced in November 1991 (and described later in this chapter), take effect. One of the booming regions is the industrial center of Guadalajara, capital city of the state of Jalisco. Sometimes described as "Mexico's Silicon Valley," Guadalajara has welcomed important new investments from IBM, Hewlett-Packard, Motorola, and a host of other electronics firms, all bringing new technologies to Mexico. U.S. automakers are also expanding their facilities in Mexico; for example, Ford Motor Company has made a $1 billion investment in a state-of-the-art car plant in Hermosillo, Sonora, in northern Mexico. The Japanese firm Nissan is making a similar-sized investment in Aguascalientes, the capital of the central Mexican state of that name. Other Japanese automakers are planning extensive new investments as well.

These developments are occurring largely because the Mexican government not only has modified foreign investment rules, but also now actively invites and encourages such investment from sources around the world. There is no surer way to signal openness to private investment than the privatization of previously state-owned or -controlled industries, and under President Salinas this activity has swung into high gear: When Salinas took office, there were 1,150 state enterprises; in early 1992 there were 200, and the Mexican government had obtained more than $14 billion from the sale of government-owned operations.

The flagship of the privatization effort was the state-owned telephone system *Teléfonos de México,* which was sold to a group of private Mexican, American, and European investors for $4 billion—one of the largest privatizations in the world. Following *Teléfonos* in importance are the former private banks of Mexico, abruptly seized by President López Portillo in 1982 but now being returned to private hands, with proceeds from their sale expected to add an additional $7 billion to government revenues. For example, the former head of the Mexican Stock Exchange put together a group of Mexican investors to buy the small *Multibanco Mercantil de México* for about $300 million. A controlling interest in Mexico's two largest banks, the *Banco Nacional de México* (Banamex) and the *Banco de Comercio* (Bancomer) were sold subsequently to private investors for some $2 billion and $3 billion, respectively. The plan is to integrate these banks into existing stock-brokerage and insurance companies to create universal, all-purpose financial institutions that, after the signing of NAFTA, can compete for customers in the United States and Canada. Plans are already underway for these Mexican "universal banks" to expand their activities into the American Southwest—particularly Texas, New Mexico, and Arizona—as soon as the necessary agreements can be negotiated.

In addition, Mexico's currency is much more stable than in the past. A policy of announced, tiny daily devaluations against the dollar ensures virtual day-to-day exchange-rate stability and keeps Mexican exports competitive while continuing Mexico's *de facto* link to the dollar.

Finally, the investment boom reflects international business confidence brought about not only by the two nations' determined moves toward economic confederacy (see Chapter 8), but also by the high quality of Mexico's economic cabinet and the apparent irreversibility of the historic economic reforms presidents de la Madrid and Salinas have undertaken.

OIL REMAINS A SENSITIVE ISSUE

Despite the recent opening of much of their economy, Mexicans are still reluctant to surrender the state's primacy in oil and gas exploration and exploitation. Mexicans, whose country's estimated reserves of 70 billion barrels represent the largest undeveloped oil fields outside the Middle East and the former Soviet Union, are proud of President Lázaro Cárdenas's nationalization of the oil industry in 1938, and there is no enthusiasm for returning to the days of foreign ownership and control. So, while the state-owned Pemex is dealing cautiously to develop some relationships (drilling contracts, for example) with U.S. and other oil companies, it would be both dramatic and unexpected if President Salinas, say, under the rubric of a North American common energy policy, were at some future point to undertake the constitutional changes necessary to invite foreign companies to participate directly in the exploration and exploitation of Mexico's oil and gas resources.

Meanwhile, the links between Pemex and international financial institutions are growing. For example, in 1991 Pemex obtained a $1.6 billion loan from the U.S. Export-Import Bank to finance U.S.-origin oil equipment and services needed to boost production. Apparently, Mexico's oil policy experts have concluded that Mexico needs to increase its surge capacity to profit from unexpected world situations like the Gulf crisis of 1990–91. Petroleum exports are already important to the Mexican economy, bringing in $8 billion in earnings in 1991. But Mexico's annual oil production of 2.7 million barrels per day, half of which is exported (with the U.S. as the biggest customer), could be much greater. With the Ex-Im Bank loan and other assistance, including a half-billion-dollar investment from Japan's Mitsui group, plans are underway to prepare Mexico for a more flexible strategy in times of sudden oil price increases.

A PARALLEL PROCESS OF POLITICAL REFORM

As described in more detail in Chapter 4, the economic reforms of the Salinas administration have been accompanied by political movement as well: the election of a conservative PAN governor of Baja California Norte; new elections in disputed gubernatorial races in Guanajuato, San Luis Potosí, and Tabasco; reform of electoral laws; greater political diversity in the Mexican Congress; and the arrest and bringing to trial of a number of corrupt union leaders, dishonest businessmen, and leading drug lords. In the area of social policy, the government has stimulated grassroots community development in rural and poor urban areas in large part through the PRONASOL program (see Chapter 3); strengthened the welfare safety net for unemployed urban workers; and reiterated its commitment to family planning in state clinics—a policy that has helped to reduce Mexico's annual population growth rate from 3.2 percent in 1976 to 2.0 percent in 1991. (Despite the popular view of a "population explosion" to our south, in fact Mexico's growth rate has declined substantially over the past decade or more.)

As a result of the favorable climate created by these and other factors, Mexican stocks have been buoyant, rising from a base 100 in 1988 to over 900 on la Bolsa de Valores (Mexican Stock Exchange Index) in January 1992.

THE MEXICAN DEBT: FROM CRISIS TO RESOLUTION

When President de la Madrid took office in 1982, Mexico's debt was, at $100 billion, the largest of any developing country in the world. Even worse, much of this debt had been negotiated when international interest rates were very high. Thus, during the de la Madrid administration, the payment of interest alone on Mexico's foreign debt amounted to a startling 6 percent of total GDP, exerting a crushing effect on public expenditures and private-sector borrowing needed to get the economy moving ahead again.

Working with foreign governments and international banks, both the de la Madrid and Salinas administrations renegotiated debt repayment down to a more manageable 2 percent of Mexican GDP. A single agreement, signed in February 1990, covered the $50 billion Mexico owed to foreign commercial banks. The agreement converted high floating interest rates to lower fixed rates, in the bargain giving Mexico needed protection from future rises in world interest rates. This freed up some $6 billion in funds for infrastructure and other investments to promote Mexico's economic growth.

With the February 1990 and subsequent agreements, Mexico is now considered by foreign financial experts to have resolved its series of debt crises, and is once again eligible for new, development-oriented lending. This invigorated relationship with the international financial community has triggered a rebound in confidence among Mexican investors, who during the 1990–92 period have returned several billion dollars in repatriated capital (which had fled the country during the disaster years of López Portillo) for new private-sector investments in Mexico's future.

But most importantly, perhaps, a stable financial situation is a strong lure to foreign investors, who can bring with them new technologies and management techniques Mexico needs if it is to compete in international trade. While it is surely in the enlightened self-interest of the United States to assist in Mexico's economic and social development in order to avoid instability

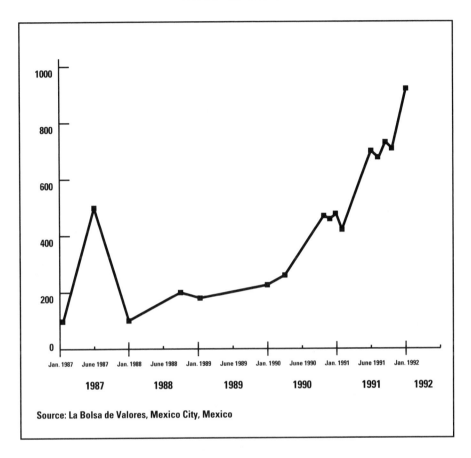

Figure 7.3
Mexico's Stock Market: Share Prices.

and to smooth the seamless web of interdependence, the hard fact remains that transnational firms, money managers, and savvy individuals make their investment decisions in a world where there is much competition from many countries for the scarce investment dollar. That is the world in which Mexico must compete, and recent economic indicators such as the 160 percent rise in the Mexican stock market in 1990–91 (see Figure 7.3) suggest that Mexico has learned to do so.

AGRARIAN REFORM IN 1992

Even Mexican and foreign observers who had become accustomed to the rapid pace of economic reforms by President Salinas since his election in 1988 were startled on November 1, 1991, when he announced at his annual *Informe*, or State of the Union address, that these reforms were coming to Mexico's politically sensitive rural area. Salinas's proposal, which required a constitutional change, granted individual ownership to the plots of land that make up *ejidos*, the community farms that were set up in the aftermath of the Revolution and have come to symbolize its material legacy to the *campesino*. The *campesinos* will in turn be allowed to sell their land to agribusinesses, which under Salinas's plan would now be able to own and operate large and economically viable farms.

President Salinas's new agrarian policies have proven to be highly unpopular with the conservative leadership within the PRI and the *caciques*, or local political chiefs, who will lose control of patronage as the *campesinos* become more indepedent of the *ejido* system. This challeges the government to prove the advantages of the new system by ensuring that the reforms result in increased employment in the rural sector (thus avoiding a further migration to the cities); providing generous agricultural credits to *campesinos* who wish to stay on the land; and, in the ongoing NAFTA negotiations, pressing Mexico's comparative advantage in producing such agricultural products as seasonal fruits and vegetables. It will probably be some time before the actual impact of the new agrarian reforms can be assessed.

Meanwhile, to understand the political impact of Salinas's proposal to reform the *ejido*, it is necessary to look more closely at the system and how it developed. It has its roots in *¡Tierra y Libertad!*—Land and liberty!—the cry of the followers of Emiliano Zapata, still a greatly admired hero of the Revolution. As the Revolution became institutionalized, the claims of the

CLINT E. SMITH

campesinos to land were translated into the *ejido* system, under which a million square kilometers (about 250 million acres) of land—though mostly marginal and not irrigated—has been distributed to more than 2 million *ejidatarios* (*campesinos* to whom land has been distributed). But while *ejidatarios* have the right to use the land, and to bequeath it to their descendants, they do not have the right to rent or sell it. In practical terms, therefore, they do not really have title to the land, and hence cannot obtain any loan against it for seeds, fertilizers, equipment, or other improvements. These must be supplied by a state agency, often controlled by corrupt local political leaders still prevalent in rural Mexico, who all too often extort the *ejidatarios*. (Hence the *caciques'* unhappiness, mentioned above, with the Salinas reforms). In any case, the *ejidatarios* operate very inefficiently, with productivity at a level far too low for competitiveness in the world market. As a result, the Mexican government has spent billions of dollars over the decades in subsidies to the 28,000 *ejidos*, and Mexico has had to import significant amounts of its grains, oils, and other items.

What President Salinas is attempting to do for the agricultural sector is what he has done in recent years for other economic sectors: make them more productive, more attractive to private investors, and more competitive in North America and the world. This proposal is seen as counterrevolutionary by such traditionalist stalwarts as Cuauhtémoc Cárdenas, whose party, the PRD, was quick to attack Salinas on the issue (and whose father was the epitome of the agrarian reformer). But, surprisingly, other criticism has been more muted, perhaps reflecting the average Mexican's perception that changes need to be made if Mexico is to play a strong and independent role in the hemispheric and world economies.

An example of these new approaches to agricultural production is a project underway in the northern state of Nuevo León, whose capital city Monterrey is a stronghold of private technological and industrial enterprise. Northern Mexico is also the heart of support for the PAN, the conservative opposition party, which strongly supports the Salinas inititative. In this project, some 300 *ejidatarios* have put up 4,000 hectares (about 10,000 acres) of land, while private investors have contributed $7 million in irrigation equipment, fertilizers, seedgrains, and modern farm machinery and the state has provided needed infrastructure improvements such as farm-to-market roads and electric-power transmission. Agricultural economists predict that the payoff from this innovative project will be substantial in 1993 and beyond, earning each *ejidatario* more than $9,000 per year and providing a 20 percent net annual return for investors. Government officials insist that this is only a single example of what is possible throughout the Mexican countryside after the proposed new reforms come into effect, probably some time in 1992. They stress that, in this and in many other cases, the *ejido* will remain intact, but will be provided with partners who can make it more productive and competitive in international markets.

ECONOMIC PARTNERSHIP

Even at the nadir of the Mexico-U.S. economic relationship in August 1982—when the bankrupt López Portillo regime pronounced itself unable to pay its international obligations and turned to the U.S. for an emergency assistance package—U.S. officials responded favorably, clearly with an eye on the possible disruption of the international financial world that could have accompanied a Mexican default. But the economic relationship began to warm in earnest early in 1983 with the advent of President de la Madrid and his programs of stability and reform. Most recently, a remarkable personal relationship has been built by Salinas and George Bush since their first meeting as presidents-elect in November 1988. That meeting, held in

Houston, included key members of the new economic teams as well as the presidents-elect and was the precursor to frequent later discussions that have led, among other things, to the historic decision to embark, along with Canada, on the NAFTA negotiations.

President Salinas has put U.S.-Mexico foreign-policy relations on an even keel. His de-emphasis on differences of opinion—for example on Central America and the U.S. invasion of Panama in December 1990—and his support of the U.S. defense of Kuwait (though with some reservations, shared by many Americans, about Desert Storm and its inconclusive end) have permitted U.S.-Mexico economic relations to prosper as strongly as they have. The spirit of new economic partnership is manifesting itself most powerfully in the context of attempts to create a continent-spanning North American Free Trade Agreement.

Part III

The Future

8 THE NORTH AMERICAN FREE TRADE AGREEMENT

The first step toward a free-trade agreement linking the three North American nations of Canada, the United States, and Mexico was taken in 1965, when a U.S.-Canada pact provided for freer trade in automotive components between the two countries. This agreement has resulted over time in an almost complete integration of automobile component manufacture and assembly at plants located in Canada and the United States, thus accomplishing economies of scale and making the industry more competitive in world markets.

Mexico's recent liberalization of investment policies has now made that country, too, an important player in trinational automobile manufacture and assembly. As early as 1965,

Mexico's celebrated *maquiladora* industry was taking advantage of modifications in the U.S. tariff schedule to favor goods assembled in Mexico with U.S. components. U.S. tariffs apply only to the value added abroad by, for example, Mexican assembly-line labor. Intermediate products can be brought into Mexico on a duty-free basis for final, usually labor-intensive processing.

The *maquiladora*, or assembly, industry consists of plants usually located just south of the 2,000-mile U.S.-Mexico border. As can be seen from Figure 8.1, the number of Mexican *maquiladora* plants has soared from 12 in 1965 to 1,500 in 1990, and total *maquiladora* exports to the U.S. have grown from $3 million in 1965 to $2.9 billion in 1990. During this period, the number of Mexicans employed in *maquiladoras* has reached more than 400,000. These plants, which employ relatively low-wage workers (predominantly women), often provide the flexibility U.S. employers need to stay competitive in a difficult international market, permitting these companies to sustain parallel manufacturing and sales operations in the U.S. rather than moving their plants overseas.

More recently (in 1987), the U.S. and Mexico signed an agreement paving the way for mutual sector-by-sector reductions in tariffs and non-tariff barriers to trade. The agreement also established procedures for handling disputes that arise when one country, convinced that another country's government is subsidizing the production cost of an imported item, assesses a countervailing duty designed to offset the alleged subsidy. In effect, these were the first steps toward a comprehensive free-trade agreement, although few realized how far and how fast these steps would come.

Parallel to the advancing U.S.-Mexican trade negotiations, moreover, were efforts to improve trade relations between Canada and Mexico. Several accords were signed similar to those between the U.S. and Mexico covering the environment,

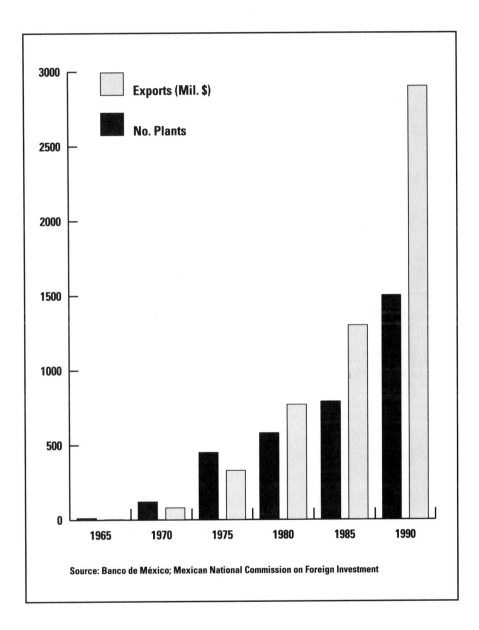

Figure 8.1
Mexican Plant and Export Growth 1965–90.

agriculture, and trade issues. Yet another trade link—one that involved intense and divisive political debate in Canada—was the signing of the United States-Canada Free Trade Agreement, which entered into force on January 1, 1989.

The pacts described above have led inevitably toward an idea whose time has come: the North American Free Trade Agreement (NAFTA). When signed and ratified, this agreement will create a market of some 360 million people with a combined output of $6 trillion—somewhat larger than that of the much-publicized European Community.

THE NORTH AMERICAN MARKET ECONOMY

In February 1991, Presidents Bush and Salinas and Canadian Prime Minister Brian Mulroney formally announced that their governments were preparing to negotiate a historic free-trade agreement, which would be a catalyst for hemispheric economic growth led by increased investment, trade, and jobs. The timing of the announcement appeared ideal for all concerned: All three countries were in need of economic stimulation—particularly the United States and Canada, which were suffering from unexpectedly persistent recessions. And although Mexico was enjoying a fairly comfortable rate of real growth thanks to recent economic reforms, its recovery was just beginning and therefore somewhat uncertain.

As talks got underway in June 1991, trade negotiators for the three countries were assigned four major tasks: 1) reduction of all tariffs to zero over the next few years; 2) elimination of pesky non-tariff barriers to North American trade; 3) ensuring an open climate for private direct investment between the three countries; and 4) full protection of intellectual property rights such as patents, trademarks, and copyrights.

Subsequent trilateral negotiations, held in various locations, have made substantial progress. To avoid dislocations to affected industries, tariffs and non-tariff barriers will be eliminated gradually over time, perhaps up to ten years. In addition, strict rules of origin will ensure that NAFTA breaks do not apply to pass-through products—essentially exports of third countries, with only nominal assembly in a NAFTA country (this rule answers criticism that Asian "maquiladoras" could be set up to circumvent NAFTA's intentions). Finally, each country will reserve the right to exclude any products that do not meet its health or safety requirements, including those involving pesticides and toxic wastes.

To be successful, NAFTA will require a strong trilateral trade mechanism, at least somewhat independent of national influences, for resolving disputes. Prototypes for such an arrangement exist in the U.S.-Canada free-trade agreement and an even earlier pact between the U.S. and Israel, both of which are focused on trade issues but could be expanded to include investment and environmental problems as well.

By the early spring of 1992, the technical aspects of the negotiations were already well along the way to a successful conclusion. That those negotiations have gone so well is quite remarkable, given Mexico's traditional desire to distance itself from the United States, past U.S. reluctance to embrace the notion of regional trade agreements, and the political debate that continues to rage within Canada about the impact of the U.S.-Canada Free Trade Agreement.

In fact, some issues are unlikely to be settled strictly on the basis of technical negotiations. Each of the three countries has a comparative advantage in the production of certain agricultural products. It is to everybody's long-term benefit that NAFTA negotiations lead to eventual free trade in agricultural products—but care must be taken along the way. For example, Canada and the U.S. can produce grains and export them to Mexico at a fraction of the cost of local production. An Iowa farmer produces eight tons of corn per hectare (2.5 acres), while a Mexican *campesino* harvests about two tons per hectare. But many very poor Mexicans depend on the sale—at a government-subsidized price double that of international prices—of the small amount of grain they grow, just to be able to purchase the bare necessities.

Clearly, some accommodation to these *campesinos*, in the form of Mexican government assistance, training programs, etc., will be essential. At the very least, changes will have to be phased in slowly and with "snapback" provisions that would allow Mexico to return temporarily to some level of protection if the rural population of Mexico needs more time to adjust to free trade in grains.

Similarly, if trade barriers were dropped, Mexico could export sugar, tomatoes, citrus fruits such as oranges, lemons, and limes, and many other fruits and vegetables (particularly in the winter) to the United States and Canada at prices below those of domestic producers. This would benefit U.S. and Canadian consumers, but here again some arrangement would have to be made to ease the transition of displaced workers to other sectors.

One of the greatest challenges to the NAFTA negotiators arises from the fact that the three economies are highly asymmetrical: The gross national product of the U.S. is about $5.3 trillion, while Canada's ($460 billion) and Mexico's ($200 billion) are far more modest. Population patterns are also quite different: The U.S. has 260 million people, Mexico 88 million, and Canada only 26 million.

But as can be seen in Figure 8.2, the aggregate figures for a North American economy are impressive: A gross product of nearly $6 trillion and a population of 362 million. These figures compare favorably with those of the European Community, which has an output of less than $5.5 trillion and a population of 350 million. A North American free-trade area might provide advantages—employment gains, higher incomes, and improved international competitiveness through production sharing,

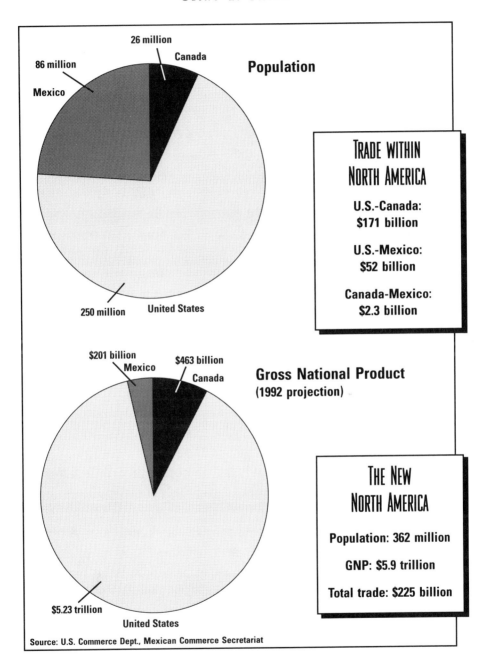

Figure 8.2
Current Populations and GNP for the U.S., Mexico, and Canada.

technology transfer, and economies of scale—equal to or better than Europe's.

NAFTA: THE BASIC ISSUES

The noisy level of political static concerning NAFTA is sure to increase as the United States gets more deeply into the election year of 1992, leading some observers to wonder whether, even if the negotiators reach an agreement in 1992, NAFTA will be submitted to Congress before early 1993. It would be wise to remind ourselves that as trade among nations becomes more free, their citizens profit from the greater variety and lower prices of the goods they purchase. The long-term benefits of free trade are not a matter of dispute among respected economists. Most analysts have concluded that the ratification of NAFTA will be good for the people of Canada, the United States, and Mexico—although the gains will not be precisely equal, given the asymmetries of trade patterns. Canada and Mexico, who each rely on the U.S. for two-thirds of their trade, would probably benefit more than the U.S., which undertakes much more of its trade with Japan and the European Community.

Short-term internal dislocations will occur as free-trade agreements are implemented, and it is the responsibility of the affected country to take these into account through social policies. Both the United States and Canada will need to provide effective labor-adjustment assistance and retrain workers affected by the removal of artificial trade barriers (in the U. S. case, against such products as steel, textiles, and glass) that have protected them in the past. In the U.S., this is provided for by the Economic Dislocation and Worker Adjustment Assistance Act (U.S. unions are quite right in insisting that displaced workers benefit from the Act's provisions); Canada has a similar law.

But the important point to remember is that the United States economy as a whole will benefit over time. To illustrate: As

Mexican real growth picked up between 1986 and 1990, Mexico's imports from the U.S. more than doubled from $13 billion to $28 billion, reaching $30 billion in 1991. Trade economists have calculated that every $1 billion in U.S. exports generates about 25,000 new domestic jobs. Thus, exports to Mexico now account for some 750,000 U.S. jobs—a welcome help in recessionary or other times. The signing of NAFTA will result in an even more rapid pace of job creation in all three countries. A recent publication of the Institute of International Economics (see Reader's Guide) predicted that some 242,000 new jobs will be created in the U.S. by increased exports resulting from NAFTA, while 112,000 workers will be dislocated by the pact, for a net increase of 130,000 jobs for American workers.

Arguably as important as new jobs is that the long-term national-security interests of the United States are best served by having neighbors who enjoy the social stability that a successful NAFTA, by stimulating growth among its members, would accomplish. A growing and stable Mexican economy is also the best, and perhaps the only, way to manage south-north migration. To complete the circle, a dynamic Mexican economy would continue to turn to the U.S. for its imports.

Economic growth and stability in Canada and Mexico benefit the United States in another way as well. Europeans have become ever more focused on economic union and on the challenge of the former Soviet Union and Warsaw Pact countries, who have shed their former associations and are turning individually or collectively to the West. At the same time, Japan is intensifying the trade and financial ties that are binding East and Southeast Asia into an emerging economic sphere. It is thus sensible for the United States and its neighbors to work closely together, though in a non-exclusionary way, to help guarantee their own export markets and economic well-being.

Mexican and Canadian expectations for NAFTA are quite similar to those of the United States, but also include the strong desire to maintain a market for their goods in the U.S. at a time when some American labor unions, threatened industrialists, and their Congressional partisans are exerting protectionist pressures. These beggar-thy-neighbor calls for trade restrictions (more often, it is true, directed against Asia) have been exacerbated by the recession and reverberate in a presidential election year like 1992. Fortunately, the din of protectionist rhetoric typically subsides after the early stages of a primary campaign, when a plethora of voices try to establish themselves—often by attempting to sound more xenophobic than their opponents.

A further advantage of NAFTA for all three countries, although particularly for Mexico, is that it will reinforce efforts to open and internationalize their domestic economies. Canada is still struggling internally for free trade among its provinces; the administrations of both de la Madrid and Salinas have worked hard to overcome Mexico's past protectionist policies. But NAFTA is much more than a trade agreement. The leaders of the three large North American countries have called for a pact that goes well beyond trade to encompass at least two other goals: improving the investment climate, and protecting intellectual property rights (patents, copyrights, and trademarks). Making the rules of the game clear and consistent in all three countries will encourage new foreign investment.

Mexico has already profited from the liberalization of foreign investment undertaken by the de la Madrid and Salinas administrations. Foreign investments in Mexico climbed from $14 billion in 1985 to more than $30 billion in 1990, and should grow even more with the signing of NAFTA. Likewise, agreed-upon protections for intellectual property will place Mexico in a much stronger position to attract investment from, say, a start-up firm spun off from Silicon Valley, which can transfer technology without fear of the theft of its patents. Companies have been understandably reluctant to enter a market where their programs are inadequately protected.

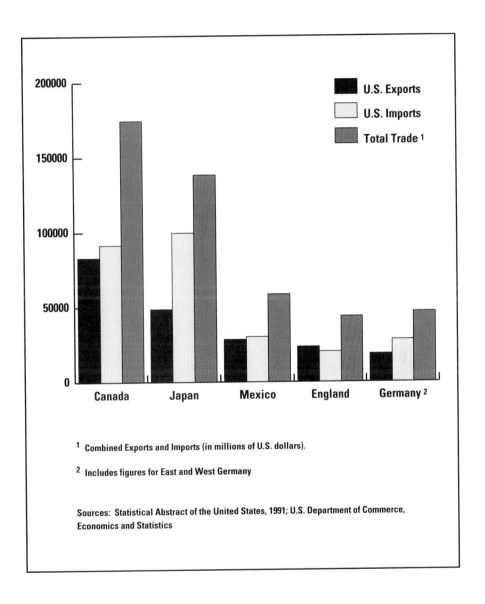

¹ Combined Exports and Imports (in millions of U.S. dollars).

² Includes figures for East and West Germany

Sources: Statistical Abstract of the United States, 1991; U.S. Department of Commerce, Economics and Statistics

Figure 8.3
Leading U.S. Trading Partners (in millions of U.S. dollars).

CANADA AND THE NAFTA DEBATE

Canada's decision to participate in NAFTA was, initially at least, a rather negative one: It joined in the discussions mainly because it felt it could not afford to be left out. The hesitation was understandable. Following the signing of the U.S.-Canadian trade pact, both countries had fallen into a recession, and many of Prime Minister Mulroney's domestic critics found it effective (however unfair) to blame him and "his" trade agreement for Canada's current economic woes. Studies by the Royal Bank of Canada and other respected sources showing that the U.S.-Canada agreement had in fact ameliorated the Canadian recession did little to quiet Mulroney's persistent detractors.

Furthermore, a free-trade agreement forces a careful look at internal economic structures, which in Canada's case are based on fragile relationships among quarreling provinces. Under those circumstances, it is understandable that the trade agreement would come under ideological fire, especially from those Canadians who see it as a move toward an undesirable convergence with an unwelcome neighbor—the often-criticized colossus to the south.

Other Canadians, however, recognize the advantages of a tripartite trade accord as opposed to the idea of the U.S. negotiating and signing separate agreements with Mexico and, perhaps, other Western Hemisphere countries—a so-called "hub and spoke" arrangement that would give only the U.S. free access to all markets and the accompanying benefits.

NAFTA AND THE ENVIRONMENT

Responsible groups are questioning the impact NAFTA might have on their country's, and the world's, environment. In fact, environmentalists have been involved in parallel discussions almost since the NAFTA negotiations were announced. One way of ensuring that economic growth following the agreement remains sustainable and environmentally healthy might be the creation of a joint commission through which Canadian, American, and Mexican environmentalists and policymakers could address international environmental issues.

For their part, the Mexicans have made it clear that they have no intention of inviting investment in plants that do not comply with environmental standards set in Mexico's 1988 comprehensive law. Based on similar U.S. legislation, this law sets high standards for new industries—and these standards, including the requirement for environmental-impact reports on new industrial construction, are being enforced. Since the passage of the 1988 law, the Mexican government has closed down more than 1,000 polluting companies, including Mexico's largest oil refinery at Azcapotzalco in Mexico City. Mexico is investing billions of dollars in a program to phase out leaded gasoline and to equip public-service vehicles with catalytic converters. While much needs to be done—in all three North American nations—there is no doubt that Mexico is taking environmental concerns very seriously and is acting, within its budget constraints, to meet international standards.

In any case, the three signatory countries retain their rights to safeguard the environment by excluding products that do not meet health or safety standards and by prohibiting trade in endangered species. In negotiations parallel to the NAFTA talks, the U.S. and Mexico are 1) designing and implementing an integrated border environment plan covering air and water pollution, hazardous wastes, chemical spills, and pesticides; 2) holding talks on the phasing in and enhancement of environmental standards; 3) jointly investigating suspected border environmental violators; and 4) planning the establishment of a high-level consultation mechanism to address environmental and conservation issues, both present and future.

163

CONFUSING INTERNATIONAL NEGOTIATIONS WITH INTERVENTION

One of the most disturbing aspects of the initiation of the trilateral trade negotiations was the insistence by some that the U.S. government use its perceived economic "leverage" stemming from these negotiations to force Mexico to institute structural changes in its internal political system. Amazingly enough, among those making these suggestions were members of Mexico's opposition parties, whose spokesmen visited the United States in the early months of the negotiations and urged, among other things, that a condition precedent to the trade talks should be Mexico's agreement that foreigners be allowed to monitor local Mexican elections!

This approach is problematic: Trade negotiations are not something exclusively beneficial for Mexico, which is therefore not in a position to be pressured by a negotiating partner. But more importantly, such attempted pressure by the U.S. would constitute an open intervention in Mexico's internal affairs and would serve only to damage relations, as such intervention has so often in the past.

THE ROOTS OF OPPOSITION TO NAFTA: AN ASSESSMENT

It is worthwhile to differentiate between the perfectly valid concerns expressed about NAFTA and some deeper, underlying malaise that has come to color the discussion. In addition to such questions as the provisions for U.S. workers displaced by NAFTA, there are other important matters that must be addressed on the environmental side: minimizing domestic and transboundary pollution of air and water by burgeoning border industries; ensuring that exported items are safe to use; etc. These questions, if properly handled, will be resolved over time, especially as economic growth provides Mexico with the resources needed for environmental protection on the scale of an industrialized country.

The fact is, however, that none of these issues, important as they are in their own right, are the ones that at the end of the day constitute the root causes of the sometimes vehement opposition to NAFTA. What are these underlying issues? Why, for example, has the AFL-CIO virtually declared war on NAFTA and opposed so strongly the Bush administration's request, subsequently granted by Congress, for "fast track" authority to conduct the negotiations? (This authority enables the U.S. special trade representative to negotiate an agreement that Congress must then either approve or reject in its entirety. Without fast track, negotiations become virtually impossible.)

Certainly one reason is the incredible frustration many Americans feel when they observe the apparent decline of American competitiveness in the marketplace and the influx of foreign products—typically from Asia or Europe—accompanied by news of foreign investments in high-profile American institutions such as Rockefeller Center or various motion picture studios. Fears about trade deficits and about America's becoming a major debtor nation are widespread, if sometimes exaggerated. The temptation exists to blame foreign influences and retreat into a populist, nationalistic "America First" mentality. If foreigners are really to blame for our problems, negotiating a trade agreement with our neighbors makes little sense!

But reality is quite different. If America has lost its competitive edge, it is because of our own domestic economic and social policies, or the lack of them, and not because of "foreigners"— least of all our Canadian and Mexican neighbors. It is beyond the scope of this book to explore America's competitive decline at any length, but there are many other easily verifiable reasons. Here are a few of them: We have made inadequate resources available for our decaying infrastructure—highways, bridges, dams, railroads, mass transportation, urban centers; we are the only industrialized nation in the world without basic health care for all our citizens; we have a higher proportion of poor children than any other developed country. The list goes on and on.

For example, six million American children live in poverty. As a nation, we have not provided the essential health care and social services needed to prevent unwanted teenage pregnancy. We have failed to provide preschool care for toddlers or Head Start programs for millions of underprivileged children of all ethnicities. We have let our public education system decline and consequently have sent millions of functionally illiterate youths into the workplace (sadly, our high-school graduates are also lacking in adequate mathematical skills). The first generation of "crack babies" is straining even further the feeble structure of public education. Thus, prospects are exceedingly dim that we will be able to make early progress in improving the achievement levels of America's students. More likely, we will continue over the foreseeable future to send poorly trained graduates to join an increasingly less competitive workforce.

We can hope that, in the long run, improved U.S. competitiveness will be accomplished primarily by addressing some of these compelling problems head-on. In the interim, we are wrong to blame "foreigners" for our troubles, and, by so doing, deny ourselves the considerable advantage on the world trade scene to be gained by a successful negotiation and enactment of NAFTA.

NAFTA'S GLOBAL IMPLICATIONS

It is not the intention of the U.S., Canadian, and Mexican negotiators that a successful NAFTA be seen as a challenge to international free trade, or to the good economic relations all three countries enjoy with the rest of the world. Indeed, it is explicit that NAFTA will adhere to all the procedures and safeguards of the GATT, which has played such a vital role in the healthy surge in world trade during the post–World War II era.

All parties concerned realize that regional free-trade agreements are always a second best to global free trade. The U.S. and its North American partners have made clear their determination to join with other GATT members to try to conclude successfully the current Uruguay Round of GATT negotiations, which are foundering on such issues as protection of intellectual property, barriers to trade in services (insurance, for instance), and, most importantly, European subsidies and protectionism regarding agricultural products.

Similarly, the North American negotiators have expressed their interest in opening NAFTA to other trading nations. This openness has gone a long way to allay fears of a "Fortress North America" expressed by some who fear that regional trade agreements are antithetical to the global system. For better or worse, such regional blocs (Europe is but the most advanced example) are a part of the world scene; the question is no longer whether they should exist, but how they can best be managed in light of the goal of freer world trade.

After NAFTA is off and running, other Western Hemisphere countries will undoubtedly voice a growing interest joining NAFTA and participating fully in its benefits. Several Central American, Caribbean, and South American countries (notably Chile) already have done so, encouraged by President Bush's Enterprise for the Americas inititiative, which promises trade benefits to Western Hemisphere countries that undertake economic restructuring and reform. Such reform is necessary to a successful free-trade arrangement; it was Mexico's decision some years ago to open its economy that made NAFTA feasible. Given the will to reform on the part of Latin American leaders, by the early years of the next century a Western Hemisphere Free Trade Agreement could be a reality.

PREPARING FOR THE 21ST CENTURY

Canada, the United States, and Mexico share a continent and are bound together by a complex web of economic and social transactions that occur millions of times a day in the interlocking worlds of trade, finance, tourism, education, and culture. The question is not, as some would wish, whether or not our interdependence is going to continue to grow. It will. The question, rather, is whether we as a North American community can guide this growing interrelationship in a way that most benefits all of our peoples.

A first test of that ability will be the successful conclusion of the North American Free Trade Agreement. A well-designed NAFTA would provide a foundation for stronger continental cooperation in many other areas of economic and social development, the environment, and migration. On the economic side, for example, informal working groups are already looking at the possibility of a North American currency accord, whereby the Mexican peso and the Canadian dollar would be linked (either firmly or within small, flexible limits) to the U.S. dollar. Such a program, however distant it may be, would encourage trade by reducing price uncertainties on the part of importers and exporters; increase foreign investors' confidence, thus enlarging financial markets; and encourage greater cooperation among Canadian, American, and Mexican authorities in achieving more-rational macroeconomic policies. Experts conclude that although a currency linkage is not necessary for a successful free-trade arrangement, it could add perceptibly to the advantages of the agreement.

After NAFTA provides relatively free trade in goods, promotes investment, and ensures intellectual property rights, what is the next economic area to be explored? A good candidate is the free flow of labor. The benefits of free movement for labor would be substantial, but, for political and other reasons described in Chapter 6, the process of integration is likely to be protracted. In such an asymmetrical labor market as North America's, the most important factor to keep in mind is that free labor movement, like free trade, is not a zero-sum game, where one side's advantage is at the cost of another. Rather it is part of a positive-sum game, in which trade, investment, and labor flows combine to produce greater productivity and higher standards of living for all.

The U.S. already benefits unilaterally from what Stanford University economist Clark W. Reynolds calls "silent integration" with Mexico through both legal and undocumented labor migration, especially in the service industries (restaurants, hotels, service stations), agriculture, and small-scale manufacturing operations. But the benefits would be greater, and more mutual, if this labor-pool integration were to be legitimized by formal intergovernmental agreements facilitating the flow of human resources in both directions; that is, not only would the more traditional south-north labor flows be rationalized, but also the more-developed partners—Canada and the U.S.—would more easily be able to send research-and-development specialists to work with Mexican counterparts in product design, worker training, quality control, and environmental-impact studies.

Economic issues, although they are given the greatest weight in the discussions about NAFTA, are not the only—nor even in the long run, perhaps, the most important—link in the North American relationship. We also need to create better understanding among the peoples of the three nations. A North American Academic Common Market—with free movement of educators and students among educational institutions in Canada, the U.S., and Mexico; common admission requirements; and enhanced transferability of academic credits—could transform the continent's knowledge base. Public resources and private philanthropy could organize and underwrite a vastly increased program of scholarships and other support for a North American educational enterprise. The resulting dense network of educational exchanges, visiting scholars, and collaborative research on North American economic and social problems would inform the vision of an emerging North American community.

These efforts should be joined in by policymakers and businessmen who would add a different dimension to the study of emerging issues in the relationship. A new generation of journalists, schooled in the affairs of all three countries, could bring a new understanding to their reporting in the electronic and print media of the transforming events of the coming decades.

All this can and should be accomplished by strengthening, not diminishing, cultural identities. The era of the "melting pot" is long behind us; each of the nations of North America enjoys a rich diversity *within* its own borders. As a whole, North America forms a fascinating mosaic of languages, literature, music, art, and aspirations. The future lies in our ability to accommodate—and celebrate—our cultural pluralism while forming a mutually beneficial civil and political society.

READER'S GUIDE

I would encourage interested readers of this book to extend their knowledge of Mexico, United States–Mexico relations, and the emerging North American community by going directly to the publications listed below by chapter. These are selected from the principal English-language sources I relied on as background material in writing this volume. I commend them to you.

Introduction and General Background

- Bilateral Commission on the Future of U.S.-Mexico Relations, *The Challenge of Interdependence: Mexico and the United States*, University Press of America, 1989.

- Pastor, Robert, and Jorge Castañeda, *Limits to Friendship: The United States and Mexico*, Knopf, 1988. (Paperback edition by Vintage/Random House, 1990.)

- Paz, Octavio, *Labyrinth of Solitude*, Grove Press, 1985.

- Reynolds, Clark W., and Carlos Tello (eds.), *U.S.-Mexico Relations: Economic and Social Aspects*, Stanford University Press, 1983.

- Roett, Riordan (ed.), *Mexico and the United States: Managing the Relationship*, Westview Press, 1988.

- Weintraub, Sidney, *Marriage of Convenience: Relations Between Mexico and the United States*, Oxford University Press, 1989.

Chapters 1–3

• Kandell, Jonathan, *La Capital: The Biography of Mexico City*, Random House, 1988. (Paperback edition by Henry Holt, 1990.)

• Cline, Howard F., *The United States and Mexico*, Harvard University Press, 1953.

• Haber, Stephen, *Industry and Underdevelopment: The Industrialization of Mexico, 1890–1940*, Stanford University Press, 1989.

• Meyer, Michael, and William L. Sherman, *The Course of Mexican History*, Oxford University Press, 4th ed., 1990.

• Miller, Robert Ryal, *Mexico: A History*, University of Oklahoma Press, 1985.

• Paz, Octavio, *The Traps of Faith: Sor Juana de la Cruz*, Harvard/Belknap Press, 1988.

• Vázquez Zoraida, Josefina, and Lorenzo Meyer, *Mexico-U.S. Relations: Conflict and Convergence*, UCLA Chicano Studies Research Center, Los Angeles, 1983.

Chapter 4–5

• Fagen, Richard R., and Olga Pellicer (eds.), *The Future of Central America: Policy Choices for the U.S. and Mexico*, Stanford University Press, 1983.

• Green, Rosario, and Peter H. Smith (eds.), *Foreign Policy in U.S.-Mexican Relations*, Center for U.S.-Mexican Studies, University of California at San Diego, 1989.

• Gonzalez, Guadalupe, and Marta Tienda (eds.), *The Drug Connection in U.S.-Mexican Relations*, Center for U.S.-Mexican Studies, University of California at San Diego, 1989.

• Purcell, Susan Kaufman, *Mexico in Transition*, Council on Foreign Relations, New York, 1988.

• Roett, Riordan (ed.), *Mexico's External Relations in the 1990s*, Lynne Rienner, 1991.

• Silva Herzog, Jesus, *Beyond the Crisis: Mexico and the Americas in Transition*, Americas Program, Stanford University, 1987.

Chapter 6

- Bean, Frank D., Barry Edmonston, and Jeffrey S. Passel (eds.), *Undocumented Migration to the United States: IRCA and the Experience of the 1980s*, RAND Corporation, Santa Monica, Calif., 1990.

- Cornelius, Wayne, and Jorge Bustamante (eds.), *Mexican Migration to the United States: Origins, Consequences, and Policy Options*, Center for U.S.-Mexican Studies, University of California at San Diego, 1989.

- Fix, Michael (ed.), *The Paper Curtain: Employer Sanctions—Implementation, Impact, and Reform*, Urban Institute, Washington, D.C., 1991.

- Gonzalez Baker, Susan, *The Cautious Welcome: The Legalization Programs of the Immigration Reform and Control Act*, Urban Institute, Washington, D.C., 1990.

- Ronfeldt, David, and Monica Ortiz de Oppermann, *Mexican Immigration, U.S. Investment, and U.S.-Mexican Relations*, RAND Corporation, Santa Monica, Calif., 1991.

Chapter 7

- Baer, M. Delal, and Guy F. Erb (eds.), *Strategic Sectors in Mexican-U.S. Free Trade*, Center for Strategic and International Studies, Washington, D.C., 1991.

- Falk, Pamela (ed.), *Petroleum and Mexico's Future*, 1987.

- Glade, William, and Cassio Luiselli (eds.), *The Economics of Interdependence: Mexico and the United States*, Center for U.S.-Mexican Studies, University of California at San Diego, 1989.

- Johnston, Bruce, et al (eds.), *U.S.-Mexico Relations: Agriculture and Rural Development*, Stanford University Press, 1987.

- Reynolds, Clark, *The Mexican Economy: Twentieth Century Structure and Growth*, Yale University Press, 1970.

- Thorup, Cathryn (ed.), *The United States and Mexico: Face to Face with New Technology*, Overseas Development Council, Washington, D.C., 1987.

- Weintraub, Sidney, Luis Rubio, and Alan D. Jones (eds.), *U.S.-Mexican Industrial Integration: The Road to Free Trade*, Westview Press, 1991.

Chapter 8

- Baer, M. Delal, "North American Free Trade," *Foreign Affairs*, Vol. 70, No. 4, Fall 1991.

- Erdmann, Peter (ed.), "Focus Issue: Mexico," *Columbia Journal of World Business*, Vol. 26, No. 2, New York, Summer 1991.

- Institute of the Americas, *Free Trade in the Hemisphere: U.S., Mexico, Canada, and Beyond—Is There a Strategy Which Serves All?*, La Jolla, Calif., March 1991.

- Reynolds, Clark, Leonard Waverman, and Gerardo Bueno (eds.), *The Dynamics of North American Trade and Investment: Canada, Mexico, and the United States*, Stanford University Press, 1991.

- Weintraub, Sidney, *Mexican Trade Policy and the North American Community*, Center for Strategic and International Studies, Washington, D.C., 1988.

- Weintraub, Sidney, "The North American Free Trade Debate," *The Washington Quarterly*, Vol. 13, No. 4, Autumn 1990.

ABOUT THE AUTHOR

Clint E. Smith, consulting professor of Latin American Studies at Stanford University and program officer for The William and Flora Hewlett Foundation in Menlo Park, California, teaches a popular seminar on United States–Mexico relations at Stanford's Center for Latin American Studies. As a career diplomat, he has been focusing on Latin American affairs for the better part of the past three decades. After serving in posts at the U.S. embassies in Buenos Aires, Madrid, and Mexico City as well as at the Mexican Desk in the State Department, he held the title of Counselor of Embassy for Economic Affairs in Lima, Peru, and then in Bucharest, Romania.

Smith, a native of Las Cruces, New Mexico, received a

bachelor's degree from the University of New Mexico and a master's degree in journalism from the University of California at Berkeley. He is married and has four children. An avid reader and tennis player, he travels with great frequency and is a member of the Council on Foreign Relations in New York, the American Foreign Service Association in Washington, D.C., and the Committee on Foreign Relations in San Francisco.

The Portable Stanford Book Series

This is a volume of the Portable Stanford Book Series, published by the Stanford Alumni Association. Subscribers receive each new Portable Stanford volume on approval. The following books may also be ordered, by number, on the adjoining card:

$12.95 titles
- *The Disappearing Border: U.S.-Mexico Relations to the 1990s* by Clint E. Smith (#4058)
- *Race Relations on Campus: Stanford Students Speak* by John H. Bunzel (#4062)
- *The Sleepwatchers* by William C. Dement (#4059)
- *Around California in 1891* by Terence Emmons (#4060)
- *Technology and Culture: A Historical Romance* by Barry M. Katz (#4057)
- *2020 Visions: Long View of a Changing World* by Richard Carlson and Bruce Goldman (#4055)
- *"What Is to Be Done?" Soviets at the Edge* by John G. Gurley (#4056)
- *Brief Lessons in High Technology: A Primer on Seven Fields that Are Changing Our Lives* edited by James Meindl (#4045)
- *Terra Non Firma: Understanding and Preparing for Earthquakes* by James M. Gere and Haresh C. Shah (#4030)

$10.95 titles
- *Notable or Notorious? A Gallery of Parisians* by Gordon Wright (#4052)
- *This Boy's Life* by Tobias Wolff (#4050)
- *Ride the Tiger to the Mountain: T'ai Chi for Health* by Martin and Emily Lee and JoAn Johnstone (#4047)
- *Alpha and Omega: Ethics at the Frontiers of Life and Death* by Ernlé W.D. Young (#4046)
- *Conceptual Blockbusting* (third edition) by James L. Adams (#4007)
- *In My Father's House: Tales of an Unconformable Man* by Nancy Huddleston Packer (#4040)
- *The Imperfect Art: Reflections on Jazz and Modern Culture* by Ted Gioia (#4048)
- *Yangtze: Nature, History, and the River* by Lyman P. Van Slyke (#4043)
- *The Eagle and the Rising Sun: America and Japan in the Twentieth Century* by John K. Emmerson and Harrison M. Holland (#4044)
- *The American Way of Life Need Not Be Hazardous to Your Health* (revised edition) by John W. Farquhar, M.D. (#4018)
- *Cory Aquino and the People of the Philippines* by Claude A. Buss (#4041)
- *Under the Gun: Nuclear Weapons and the Superpowers* by Coit D. Blacker (#4039)

- *50: Midlife in Perspective* by Herant Katchadourian, M.D. (#4038)
- *Wide Awake at 3:00 A.M.: By Choice or By Chance?* by Richard M. Coleman (#4036)
- *Hormones: The Messengers of Life* by Lawrence Crapo, M.D. (#4035)
- *Panic: Facing Fears, Phobias, and Anxiety* by Stewart Agras, M.D. (#4034)
- *Who Controls Our Schools? American Values in Conflict* by Michael W. Kirst (#4033)
- *Matters of Life and Death: Risks vs. Benefits of Medical Care* by Eugene D. Robin, M.D. (#4032)
- *On Nineteen Eighty-Four* edited by Peter Stansky (#4031)
- *The Musical Experience: Sound, Movement, and Arrival* by Leonard G. Ratner (#4029)
- *Challenges to Communism* by John G. Gurley (#4028)
- *Cosmic Horizons: Understanding the Universe* by Robert V. Wagoner and Donald W. Goldsmith (#4027)
- *Beyond the Turning Point: The U.S. Economy in the 1980s* by Ezra Solomon (#4026)
- *The Age of Television* by Martin Esslin (#4025)
- *Insiders and Outliers: A Procession of Frenchmen* by Gordon Wright (#4024)
- *Mirror and Mirage: Fiction by Nineteen* by Albert J. Guerard (#4023)
- *The Touch of Time: Myth, Memory, and the Self* by Albert J. Guerard (#4022)
- *The Politics of Contraception* by Carl Djerassi (#4020)
- *Economic Policy Beyond the Headlines* by George P. Shultz and Kenneth W. Dam (#4017)
- *Law Without Lawyers: A Comparative View of Law in China and the United States* by Victor H. Li (#4015)
- *The World That Could Be* by Robert C. North (#4014)
- *America: The View from Europe* by J. Martin Evans (#4013)
- *An Incomplete Guide to the Future* by Willis W. Harman (#4012)
- *Murder and Madness* by Donald T. Lunde, M.D. (#4010)
- *The Anxious Economy* by Ezra Solomon (#4009)
- *The Galactic Club: Intelligent Life in Outer Space* by Ronald Bracewell (#4008)
- *Is Man Incomprehensible to Man?* by Philip H. Rhinelander (#4005)
- *Some Must Watch While Some Must Sleep* by William E. Dement, M.D. (#4003)
- *Human Sexuality: Sense and Nonsense* by Herant Katchadourian, M.D. (#4002)